REARVIEWING SOCIAL RESEARCH

DARING CONCEPTIONS

R KUMARAN

Copyright © R KUMARAN
All Rights Reserved.

This book has been self-published with all reasonable efforts taken to make the material error-free by the author. No part of this book shall be used, reproduced in any manner whatsoever without written permission from the author, except in the case of brief quotations embodied in critical articles and reviews.

The Author of this book is solely responsible and liable for its content including but not limited to the views, representations, descriptions, statements, information, opinions and references ["Content"]. The Content of this book shall not constitute or be construed or deemed to reflect the opinion or expression of the Publisher or Editor. Neither the Publisher nor Editor endorse or approve the Content of this book or guarantee the reliability, accuracy or completeness of the Content published herein and do not make any representations or warranties of any kind, express or implied, including but not limited to the implied warranties of merchantability, fitness for a particular purpose. The Publisher and Editor shall not be liable whatsoever for any errors, omissions, whether such errors or omissions result from negligence, accident, or any other cause or claims for loss or damages of any kind, including without limitation, indirect or consequential loss or damage arising out of use, inability to use, or about the reliability, accuracy or sufficiency of the information contained in this book.

Made with ♥ on the Notion Press Platform
www.notionpress.com

For,

All the ordinary humans, who exiled and rendered irrelevant the expert in me

Contents

the planning transformations in development sector have often happened as a result of patient and democratic listening to the last human, who is always left out of this research. Hence, the papers in this book scream 'Please attention to the last human'. It seeks to reconfigure the research enterprise from the view of that last human. Indeed, if we reverse the telescope of research and learn to see from the other end of it, everything becomes completely different. That is why, in chapter 3, I pay tribute to the art of listening as a radical art in development research or in social research.

Yet, another discomfiture we have with current quantification bias of social research is that poor and poverty have so deeply been reified, that they are treated as frozen categories and *being poor has almost become a personality type.* Poor in this book will be known as *people living in poverty*, who could easily have more dimensionality of personhood, than just being poor. When we call the so-called 'poor' as people in poverty, we redeem them of the developmentalist economistic bias; and we attribute to them many other human dimensionalities, other than the economic dimension of being resource or economic poor.

Another correction, this book (chapter 4) seeks to make is on the idea of community care as opposed to collective care. There was a (and even now too) time when community care was celebrated as an important element of de-institutionalization. But, I argue in favour of collective care, (instead of community care that ended up burdening the women and aged as the primary care-givers), thereby making everybody responsible for caring for the welfare of the marginalised and excluded. The last paper in this book is asking for a new form of governance in the context of neoliberalism. All these papers have been written with more propositional spirit than with empirical spirit, as well as in the spirit of making corrections to the existing thinking in the development and social research. These papers are strongly influenced by the Gandhian spirit, asking for understanding development issues through heart instead of approaching poverty and marginalization through brain. The intended audience of this book are both development sector researchers and practitioners as well as academicians.

Marginalized people, such as people with disability, people with stigmatized identities like sexworkers, people with stigmatized ailments such as leprosy, mental illness and HIV, Dalits (particularly manual scavengers among them), transgenders, tribal people, widows, urban homeless people and prisoners and many others, have remained the most invisibilised people India, perhaps as elsewhere in the world. What is rendered invisible is not just the personalities of these marginalized people, but their life sustaining strategies, experiences, creativity and worldview as a whole. What engendered this cruel situation has a lot to do with changing conceptions of society, man(human), development and man's relationship with the world, polity etc.

While each society in some era or the other has invisibilised one or other these categories and treated them with contempt and disdain, no society has dumped *all* of them into the invisible zone like the modern contemporary society. If ever they received some attention, it was one of condescending and charitable nature that subsumed the contempt and disdain in the same virulent form as ever. This was further compounded by what even the most revolutionary reformists had theorized. Speaking as they did under the shadow of modernity they only affirmed the invisibilisation processes, for they championed the very modern values of productivity and social usefulness that marginalized these unfortunate individuals. Marxism and liberalism are examples of this line of thinking.

However, one significant voice that not only visibilized and actively sided with the marginalized and the invisibilised, but made work with them a first condition for social engagement was that of Mohan Das Gandhi, in India. It was he who, with this typical spiritual overtones, declared that God is with the poor and marginalized, and went even further to announce that God himself being that very poor person.

It was in Gandhi's ideas and action one finds scope for recognizing people for *what they are* and celebration of the very principles that are anti-thesis to modern society – values such as feminity, non-productivity, etc. it was with the strength of such perspectives that one can hope to visibilise the people condemned into the dark tunnels of society.

I

Conceptualising Poverty

"Poverty is the worst form of violence."

-Mahatma *Gandhi*

Poverty has been the central concern of development studies, since its inception. In recent years poverty has come to be understood in much more qualitative manner, than the mere quantification that characterised the early days. Now poverty is conceptualised as a multidimensional reality in terms of the absence of many qualitative elements such as dignity, empowerment and participation. Some have characterised it in in terms of what poverty entails, namely social exclusion (Arjan de Haan, 2010; Deepa Narayan, 2000; Amartya Sen, 1987). Such approaches have benefited a lot from sociological and anthropological understanding of human existence and condition, though, it must be said, that these disciplines have turned their attention to poverty only recently. These studies have a lot to learn from Gandhian understanding of society and what, according to Gandhi, constitutes human existence. All these combined together have taken the understanding of poverty from mere quantitative and output orientation to process oriented and holistic understanding.

Human Condition

In the last few decades it has become increasingly apparent that while numbers can be used to define the phenomenon of poverty, there is a need to take cognisance of other forms of knowledge and human experiences – those that cannot be so easily quantified because they deal with the human experience, such as complex set of intelligence, emotions, relationships and

"

values (see Chambers, 1997; Narayan, 2000; and Bauman, 2005). It has also become obvious to the experts that the people in poverty are not passive, lazy or foolish. On the contrary, they work hard, creatively, and continuously manage their resources to survive against odds that seem insurmountable (see Willis 1977; Collins, 2009; Scott 1979 & 1985; and Mander 2002). The count of bodies, money and calories therefore needs to be supplemented with an understanding of the embodiment of poverty and the relationships through which poverty is sustained and replicated.

Poverty is a reflection of an unequal distribution of the world's resources mediated by a complex set of inequitable human relations and transactions (Chambers 1997 and Galtung, 1996). The world's resources are collected and consumed by a few at the expense of others. Retaining most people in a state of want is not merely an act of negligence or lack of caring or political will, or even of inefficient management. It is a series of acts that impoverish or keep people poor because it pays some to keep others in a state of want (Bauman, 2005). This process of impoverishment is mediated by institutions through relationships of power that are masked by normalization of the inequitable socio-politico-cultural processes and the evasion of responsibility for the outcomes (Baxi 2003).

In the perspective of this researcher, therefore, making sure that there are no poor people in the world requires not merely a mathematical or grand redistribution of resources but a process of reflection on values that encompass the human spirit and race as a whole, and that underpin daily transactions. These values and relationships are embedded within complex locations best known to the person experiencing the situation, rather than those that are studying it. Essential to hearing the voices of the poor and seeking to work with them on platforms of equality are our own processes of self-reflexivity and institutional accountability.

This research is part of this effort. Through this, the researcher seeks to look into the lives of people in poverty to not merely understand their experiences, but also to reflect on ours, and our relation to them. Essential to this process is the willingness of the person living in poverty to share the details of his/her life – a willingness that marks his/her generosity to continue to be vulnerable even when that vulnerability has been repeatedly used against her/him and has been misrepresented by the limitations of what we want to hear and can hear. Perhaps more essential to this process is our willingness to relate to their stories as equals – one human to another.

Poverty: towards a multi-dimensional definition

In over a century of poverty research, the field is now saturated with definitions. Approaches to poverty within development discourses have been predominantly located within economic growth paradigms. At different periods in the 20th century, production, industrialization and trade have been at the focus of the debates on economic growth, with the underlying presumption that economic growth would automatically "trickle down", resulting in the reduction or elimination of poverty. However, the persistence of poverty not only in the "developing", but also in the "developed" countries required a reconsideration of this conflation between economic growth, development, and reduction of poverty. It became apparent that economic growth did not necessarily lead to social development, or reduction of poverty: i.e., a high level of economic output, technological advances, and industrialization with material wealth for some was often accompanied by the severe exploitation of labour, environmental pollution, poverty, social distress and conflict.

In the last two decades of this century, development discourses shifted to accommodate views of poverty that were beyond merely economic, and have focussed on dimensions of poverty such as inequality, human rights and entitlements. The different possible "components" of poverty definitions have been summarized by Baulch (1996) in the pyramid below, where PC or personal consumption (reflected in income and expenditure) is at one end of the uni-dimensional approach to poverty. At the multi-dimensional end is included wider concepts such as access to common property resources (CPR), state provided commodities (SPC), the ownership of assets to protect against destitution, dignity, and autonomy.

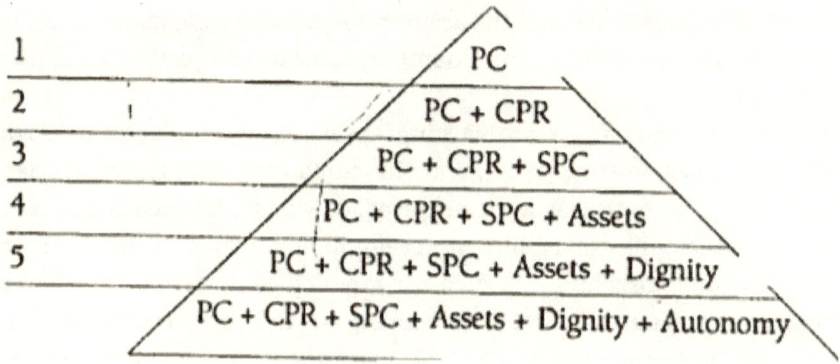

Figure 1- Pyramid of Poverty

Using this pyramid as a map, we propose to briefly discuss the following broad dimensions of poverty through the historical trajectory of theoretical and policy approaches to poverty. This research will focus on three broad development debates: modernization theory, trade theory, and human development theories. In each of the subsequent sections, there will be a discussion of the development theories and their philosophical assumptions, the implications for approaches to poverty, and the experiences of states.

High Modernization: economic growth and development

High modernization theory can be described as the view that economic growth and development is a consequence of a self-reinforcing "virtuous" circle of industrialization. The simple version is described by Rosenstein-Rodan's (1943) "Big Push" theory in which he argues that modern methods of production are potentially better than traditional ones, but their productivity edge is large enough to compensate for the necessity of paying higher wages only if the market is large enough. However, the size of the market depends on the extent to which modern techniques are adopted, because workers in the modern sector earn higher wages and/or participate in the market economy more than traditional workers. So if industrialization can be started on a sufficiently large scale, it will be self-sustaining, but it is possible for an economy to get caught in a "vicious" cycle in which the process never gets going. The theory makes the assumption of economies of scale, i.e., that the factory must be established at an appropriately large scale, and the assumption of economic dualism i.e., that the workers can be drawn from unemployment or low paying agricultural employment.

Within this central vision, varying emphases were placed by Arthur Lewis [1954, 1955], Rostow [1960], and Hirschman [1958] in their theories of how economic growth was to be achieved. Lewis emphasized the potential of unlimited supplies of labour in developing countries. In his "Balanced Growth" model, Hirschman argued for a policy of investing in a few key sectors with strong linkages, then moving on to other sectors to correct the disequilibrium generated by these investments. Rostow articulated an historical perspective, making an argument for four "Stages of Development", which developing countries would have to pass through in order to eventually "catch up" with the developed countries (Rostow, 1960).

Planned Development and the Welfare State

In the aftermath of World War II, the newly independent, former colonies tackled the question of economic development with the tool kit of developed nations. However, these countries were characterised by a shortage of capital, and the new governments had to balance on the one hand the need to divert a part of the of the country's available resources to expand production in the future, and on the other hand, to address the immediate needs of the those living in poverty. Inspired by the Soviet example, these countries viewed state intervention as an essential strategy to balance both requirements through planned economic growth along with welfare. Although the concept of the "Developmental State" was not new (Marx, List, and other political economists had theorized it) the development states that evolved in the third world were, however, distinct from both the Soviet command economy model and the typical liberal democratic market oriented model of Europe and North America.

The focus of these new states was on industrial production based on import substitution with protective tariffs. It stemmed from the ideas that first, reduction in poverty or the improvement in living standards depended on improvement in the productive capacity of a people. Second, that an export based economy would not be able to compete with developed countries. Third, that technical progress in agriculture would lead to labour surplus and therefore a shift from agricultural to industrial production.

In Lipton and Maxwell's (1995) taxonomy of state approaches to poverty, the newly independent countries in the 1950s relied on community development. During the 1960s, it was expected that intensification of agricultural inputs (particularly hybrid seeds, fertilizer and mechanization technologies) would effect the desired transformation of rural economies. By the 1970s, it became apparent that this "trickle down" approach to poverty alleviation was ineffective, and that direct transfers to the poor were necessary. Poverty alleviation programmes began to focus on integrated rural development, rural credit, and basic needs.

The strategy of state-led development fell into disfavour by the mid-70s because of the widening foreign exchange gap, and the failure to achieve levels of economic growth that resulted in the reduction of poverty. It also become apparent that the development state apparatus was controlled (to varying degrees in different countries) by coalitions of elite groups made up of bureaucrats, politicians, the military, and industrialists. Some combinations, as in South-east Asia (epitomized by the techno-bureaucrat and industrialist collaboration in the *chaebols* of Korea) produced the desired economic growth rates. In contrast, deepening crises of poverty and inequality were the result of such elite group manoeuvres in many countries of Latin America and Africa. It is only recently that attempts have been made to conceptualize these differences in the conditions and characteristics of development states. The shift is from treating the state as a "rational, efficient, neutral bureaucratic institution", towards recognizing that its functioning is mediated by *political* compulsions (Leftwich, 1995).

Approaches to Poverty: absolute and relative definitions of economic well being

Given the co-relation between well-being and commodity consumption/production within the modernization paradigm of the welfare state, absolute poverty is conceptualized as the lack of a basic level of income to achieve a given level of consumption. Measures of poverty within this frame are of levels of income, expenditure, and nutritional intake; however, there is much disagreement on what could be considered adequate level of consumption or income for survival. The UNDP, for instance has defined absolute deprivation as those with less than one dollar a day of income.

This definition has been expanded to include the "inability to obtain a minimum standard of living" i.e., to have enough resources to meet basic bodily requirements. The ILO's Basic Needs approach that focussed on education, nutrition and health is based on a moral imperative to prioritize the minimum requirement for a "decent life", and as such, though it shifts the focus from income-based measurements of poverty, is still an absolute construct (Stewart, 1995). Chronic hunger, ill health and homelessness are the physical manifestations of this absence of income. Many definitions of poverty are of conditions where basic needs for survival are unfulfilled: primarily food, but also good health, shelter and clothing. The poor do not eat enough, live in makeshift shelters and usually have no protection from the elements. The UNDP (2000) differentiates between the inability to meet basic food needs (extreme, absolute poverty), and the inability to meet non-food needs.

Most nations define poverty through per capita income, caloric intake and other statistical indicators. This definition of poverty through resources consumed/produced at the subsistence level is the foundation for the construction of the "poverty line" and for designing poverty alleviation policy in most countries.

Absolute definitions of poverty (whether of income or of basic needs) are static, uni-dimensional descriptions, with no insights about the complexity of the person's experience, the processes that created the condition or the processes that could alleviate it. The income and wellbeing definitions of poverty implicitly locate *agency* for poverty within the poor person. That is, people are poor because of their *personal inadequacy* to create and manage enough resources that will move them into a better life position. Policy solutions are reflected in state resource transfers, through welfare and relief programmes that focus on the fulfilment of the basic needs of the individual.

Concepts of relative poverty were developed initially in the countries of the North, since it was apparent that although people were not in absolute poverty, they were poor relative to others in that society i.e., they are a measure of income distribution. These measures are dependent on the countries' wealth, and commonly now in developed countries, the poverty line is set at a level of half the median national income (Wagle, 2001). However, as Sen (1983:157) points out, while the stated intent of relative poverty measures is to capture income inequalities, such measures run the risk of obscuring a general intensification of poverty that can affect rich and poor alike.

Welfare measures or the "policy definitions" of poverty are also a relative measure: they are the scales used by the U.S and U.K governments to determine welfare benefits that the state should minimally provide to all citizens. There are two dangers inherent in such a circular definition: first, the contradiction that if the poor are defined by the level of welfare benefits, the most effective "poverty reduction" strategy would ostensibly be to reduce the benefits. Second, since the determination of the poverty line is not linked to actual poverty, but to policy objectives (what the state should minimally provide), it is subject to political pressures (Sen, 1983: 158).

Underlying Assumptions and critique

The philosophical assumptions of modernization theories continue to be powerfully embedded in most mainstream development discourses and by extension, poverty discourses. These include universalizing assumptions about rational economic behaviour, the need for 'optimum allocation of scarce resources', maximization of utility etc. These are premises shared regardless of whether the political ideology is Marxist, or anywhere else on the spectrum to conservative. The administrative ordering of the modernizing, planned development State assumes that the superiority of western, rational scientific methods will automatically replace an unjust social order with the egalitarian benefits of "progress" for all (Scott, 1998). Two constructions using these building blocks that have consequences for poverty are first, the inescapable, necessary linkage between well-being and commodity production/consumption. Second is the vision (pioneered by Rostow) of a linear development path that all countries will inevitably follow. This vision continues to be powerfully embedded in development discourses, as we shall see, even the "non-economic" ones.

However, the economic definition of poverty is inadequate for three key economic and non-economic reasons. First, (and within economic terrain) it does not acknowledge *inequality* is a crucial dimension of poverty.

Inequality is a *structural* determinant of poverty: traditionally, unequal access to land, resources and education (often reflected through urban bias) have determined poverty. In addition, non-traditional inequality is induced by skill based technical change, weakening of labour institutions, trade shocks, and inadequate social protection and by governments aggressively pursuing stabilisation policies (Cornia, 2000). The Gini coefficient or the measure of income inequality[1] is used along with per capita income to analyse the distribution of income within a country, and globally. Maxwell (2000, citing a little publicized, comprehensive study of country data by Milanovic in 1999) points to the fact that income gini coefficients are high and may be increasing nationally, and globally. A cause for serious concern is the inequality between rich and poor nations: the global Gini is 0.66, and in the past decade, the real income of the bottom 20% fell (there was an increase in both absolute and relative poverty globally). New analyses according to which inequality is not only bad for the poor, but bad for economic growth (Deninger and Squire, 1998) provide an economic efficiency argument against inequality, and for re-distribution. However, as this study will argue, the re-distribution agenda faces great political resistance from elites, and is on stronger grounds through a rights-based approach.

The second key dimension of poverty economic definitions occlude is *vulnerability*, a concept which challenges the arbitrariness of a "poverty line", and which points to the *transient* quality of poverty for some people, as they move in and out of poverty; while for others poverty may be a more permanent, chronic feature. State welfare provisions in the countries of the North provide a buffer in this zone of vulnerability, the withdrawal of which can lead to rapid plunges into poverty for working class and professional people, as the experience of several of the former Soviet countries demonstrates.

Finally, the third dimension of poverty not captured by economic definitions is *deprivation*, which refers to the range of rights and resources that affect people's quality of life and enable or prevent them participating fully in society. Deprivation is usually consequence of processes that create poverty; including those that circumscribe people from accessing entitlements that are not merely individual – drinking water, food, clothing and shelter; but also those that are defined by the *institutions* of society including the state – right to education, health, income-generation, etc.

There is now considerable consensus that the narrow, economic wellbeing dimensions of poverty are definitionally inadequate, and need to be expanded to include powerlessness, insecurity, vulnerability, inequality, injustice, discrimination, marginalisation and social exclusion.

Trade liberalization

The ISI (import substituting industrialization) model of the 50s and 60s was noted for its critique of free trade policies especially by the "under-development theorists", Prebisch and Gunder Frank. In particular, Frank challenged the linear version of the development path, arguing that the present of developing countries is not equal to the past of the developed countries (i.e., when latter were *undeveloped*). According to this Marxian analysis, underdevelopment is an unavoidable product of the internal contradiction of capitalist development in which the metropolitan, developed core of the national and the global economies survived by exploiting the resources (labour and material) of the rural, under-developed peripheries. In this framework, free trade was viewed as a mechanism used by the ruling classes for continued extraction of surplus value and the perpetuation even deepening, this inequality and poverty in the peripheries

(Frank, 1969).

The neo-liberal resurgence of the 1970s swept aside such reservations about trade, and ushered in a new era in which free trade is aggressively promoted, particularly by International Financial Institutions (IFIs)[2], as the vehicle of economic growth. The protectionism of the planned economies was criticized for promoting corruption and inefficient utilization of resources. According to neo-liberal trade theory, opening up an economy to trade would optimally utilize the abundant factor of production, which in developing countries is the unskilled labour of poor people. Trade liberalization is one among a range of instruments recommended by advocates of the typical IFI policy package: "Poverty reduction is best served by served by more rapid adjustment to fiscal imbalances, rapid adjustment to inflation and external deficits and the use of high interest rates to achieve these ends, internal and external sector financial sector liberalization, deregulation of capital controls, deep and rapid privatization of state owned enterprises and, perhaps the strongest unifying factor in this group [of those advocating such reforms], rapid and major opening up of an economy to trade and foreign direct investment" (Kanbur, 2001:1085)

The Market State

With the resurgence of neo-liberalism, the last decades of the 20th century were witness to the (often forced) opening up of developing country economies to trade and investment. Simultaneously, the IFI policy package of Structural Adjustment Programs (SAP) has directly and indirectly exacerbated poverty in many countries, although ostensibly, "safety nets" were to be designed for the poor to protect them from a worsening of their conditions.

The direct impact of SAP has been through the withdrawal of state resources from welfare programmes such as health, education, nutrition etc. The consequences are most severe for the poor, not only because of the loss of transfer income (from welfare benefits), but also because they are least able to substitute with market services. The indirect impact has been through liberalization policies: the loss of jobs due to retrenchment, loss of livelihoods in sectors (particularly agriculture based) that had previously been protected.

Approaches to Poverty: "Safety Nets" for the Poor

Conventional SAPs of the IFIs recommend public expenditure cuts, which initially translated into policies that directly impacted the poor: typically, the abolition/reduction of food subsidies and introduction of user charges for health and education services. Other policy changes under SAP had indirect effects on the poor, through structural changes in the economy wrought by devaluation or liberalization. "Both IFIs only acknowledged the need for a change towards policies in which protection of the poor became a central aim, three-quarters through the adjustment decade (around 1987). Actual policy changes came even later." (Stewart et. al, 1996:213)

The bitter pill of the IFI doctors has now been "sugar-coated" with the prescriptions of "safety-nets" for the poor. These include (supposedly) food subsidies, health and education provisions targeting the poor. However, analyses of adjusting country SAP policies indicate that they do not show a greater shift to even to the minimal "add on" social sector funding. Further, the funds have been mainly directed at the new poor, and do little for the chronically poor (Stewart et. al, 1996:213).

Underlying assumptions and critique

The emphasis on trade liberalization did not challenge the tightly held philosophy that growth of per capita income was the central tenet of economic development and poverty reduction: it shares the same assumptions. It did not alter the ends (economic growth), just changed the means (trade, not planned development and ISI). Kanbur (2001) looks past the impasse of oppositional rhetoric of the advocates and opponents of trade liberalization, and examines their different premises. These include assumptions about the level of disaggregation, the time horizon and the market structure. The advocates of trade liberalization point to the positive effects of growth at an aggregate level, but do not take into account the regional and group inequalities and variations, as well as the population growth rates that affect the absolute and relative incidence of poverty. Second, they assume a medium time horizon, which discounts the short-term immediate impact of SAP on the poor, who are particularly vulnerable to such shocks. It also discounts the costs of considering long-term sustainability. And finally, they assume that market structures are competitive, ignoring the segmented structure of factor markets, in which labour and capital have unequal bargaining power: i.e., the increased mobility of global corporate capital makes labour in both sending and receiving countries worse off.

Human Development

The seminal contribution of Sen's capability and entitlement approach to human development theories has been to integrate both the absolute and relative aspects of poverty; while simultaneously acknowledging the multi-dimensional character of poverty. The emphasis is not only on *being* well-nourished or educated, but more fundamentally on people's *capability* to achieve these states. Thus there is an *absolute* core of *capabilities* (or level of functioning) required to achieve command over *commodities* for survival. The set of commodities necessary for well-being would be *relative* – i.e., they may be different for different societies. A persons' entitlement is the set of commodities he or she has the capability to command within the legal framework of their society – either directly (through production), or indirectly (through exchange of labour, assets; or through state transfers etc.). Within this framework, poverty is a failure of entitlements, not merely the failure to possess the commodities required for survival (Sen, 1985).

The capability definition of poverty is based on a more dense and complex recognition of poverty as a multi-dimensional phenomenon. Amartya Sen's "Capability Framework" addresses basic needs fulfilment (such as education, nutrition and health), as well as the aspects of poverty that the economic definitions fail to capture; namely, inequality, vulnerability and deprivation. "There is an irreducible core of absolute deprivation in our idea of poverty, which translates manifestations of death by starvation, malnutrition and visible misery into a diagnosis of poverty, without first looking into the relative panorama. Thus the approach of relative deprivation complements rather than replaces the analysis of poverty in terms of absolute deprivation. Poverty is understood to be an absolute concept in the space of capacities and achievements, and relative in terms of goods and satisfiers."[3]

This analysis of poverty as a "quality of life" is a composite definition of poverty that allows for a major shift from the exclusive focus on the poor person's well being (defined in absolute terms) to the concept of individual *functioning*, or capabilities to achieve well being (defined in relative terms). Thus, the commodities required for well being could be relative, but the capacities (good health, education) to attain them would be absolute. Central to this framework are two key concepts: that of poor people's *entitlements* to land, livestock, common property resources, or state welfare provisions; as well as human dignity and freedom.

In this framework, poverty is a state in which freedom of choice does not exist. Necessity lies at one end of the continuum and preference at the other wherein the former is involuntary, while the latter is voluntary. Human needs cannot be merely circumscribed around the needs of the body. The need of the human spirit for dignity, self-respect and happiness, for a life that is free and non-violated also becomes important to articulate.

The elaboration of the discourse on poverty and human development has been greatly influenced by Sen's theory, as well as Dasgupta's conceptualization of well-being (1989, 1990). Well-being goes further, and includes indices of political and civil rights, which he argues, are co-related with the improvement of life expectancy, infant mortality and per capita income (Dasgupta, 1990:4).

"Virtuous" and "Vicious" States

Poverty reduction re-emerged on the international agenda in 1990, with the publication of the World Bank's *World Development Report* on poverty, and the UNDP's *Human Development Report* (HDR). The latter defined human development as "enlarging peoples' choices"; to enable them to live longer, healthier and fuller lives (UNDP, 1990). Central to the HDR's shift in emphasis from per capita GNP is the Human Development Index (HDI) which is a composite measure of poverty based on measures of life expectancy, schooling and income.

The HDI was extended by the Gender Development Index (GDI) measuring gender disparities, and the Human Poverty Index (HPI) which provides a disaggregation of the percentage of people who suffer from deprivation. However, it has to be noted, that although the HDI and GDI expand the concept of poverty beyond economic criteria, there are some limitations: first, they are absolute measures, and therefore do not necessarily describe relative deprivation or variations (by group, gender, region, etc.), especially within a country.

Further, taken together, although the HDRs up to 2001 make a case for human development, there are several ambiguities in the articulation of linkages between human development and economic growth. Economic growth continues to be implicitly important, but there is vagueness in its conceptualization (Ravaillion, 1997). On the one hand, there is the explicit call for strong public action to counter the ills of economic growth, particularly the concurrent increase in unemployment and inequality. On the other hand, there is a continued lack of clarity on the sequencing (if any) between economic growth and human development.

Stewart and Ranis (2000) propose a conceptualization that offers a potentially useful integration of both concepts by centring HD and showing the importance of EG as a tool for achieving it. Their cross-country analysis shows that there are "virtuous" and "vicious" spirals of development in which HD and economic growth have mutually re-enforcing effects:

"Country performance can be usefully classified into four categories: virtuous, vicious and 2 kinds of lop-sidedness: i.e., lopsided with strong HD/weak growth (called HD-lopsided); and lopsided with weak HD/ strong growth (called EG lop-sided)" (Stewart and Ranis, 2000:208)

Using this framework, they classify developing countries paths across three decades: thus, for e.g., many of the Latin American countries are HD-lopsided and Chile has moved into a virtuous cycle. Several of the South-East Asian economies are in virtuous cycles, but the Philippines has moved from HD lopsided to EG lopsided to vicious. In South Asia, Sri Lanka has the distinction of being in virtuous cycles; and most of the African countries are stuck in vicious cycles of development. These cycles are dependent on the levels of inequality in the country at the outset, the public expenditure choices of states, and the degree of women's control over intra-household resource allocation. Their conclusion is that policy is an iterative process, which must begin with a focus on HD cycles before economic growth can be achieved, and conversely, that economic growth cycles will not be sustainable in the long run if HD is ignored.

Approaches to Poverty: "Attacking poverty"?

The perspective shift recognizing the multi-dimensionality of poverty is made by the World Bank in the latest World Development Report 2000-2001: Attacking Poverty (World Bank, 2000). The report process engaged in an unprecedented wide-ranging, participatory consultative exercise with development practitioners, policy makers, and directly with the poor in 23 countries, producing the volumes Voices of the Poor: Can Anyone Hear Us? ; and Voices of the Poor: Crying out for Change (Narayan et. al, 2000a, 2000b).

International commitment to poverty reduction has received additional strong impetus from the OECD's Development Assistance Committee (DAC) Targets, which were re-iterated at the UN Millennium Summit in 2000 and agreed upon by 189 member states. The key targets to be achieved by 2015[4] are to:

- Halve extreme poverty
- Reduce infant mortality by two-thirds, and maternal mortality by three-fourths
- Universalize primary education in all countries
- Reverse trends in loss of environmental resources nationally and globally

Significantly, there was recognition that poverty was not merely a national issue, but a global moral imperative. There was agreement on five minimum policies to achieve these targets that included increase in foreign aid commitments, trade policies supportive of developing countries (i.e., remove tariff and non-tariff barriers and agricultural subsidies in North countries), deeper debt relief, and a global AIDS and health fund.

Underlying assumptions and critique

However, the capability framework has its limitations: first, it tends to use the indicators of well-being – i.e., morbidity, life expectancy and education - as proxy indicators of capabilities (since these affect well-being directly, and indirectly in terms of the *capability* to improve well-being). Second, the focus is, on individuals, and entitlements are primarily configured vis-à-vis the state. Social institutions such as gender, caste, ethnicity and religion; the market are major non-formal arbiters of entitlements.

"Sen's entitlement analysis marginalises non-governmental sites of rule-making and rule-enforcing which affect entitlement by either downplaying the role of socially enforced moral rules, or compartmentalising them to the domestic sphere. As a consequence, the interplay between the working of socially enforced moral rules and the working of state enforced legal rules in determining a person's entitlement is ignored" (Gore, 1993:444).

The experience of poverty is mediated by both the identity of the person and the institutions within which the person operates and negotiates. This experience of poverty is also seen as a relational aspect – in comparison with others and in comparison across time – past and future and in comparison with an ideal state of existence. The definition moves from being absolute to being relational, from being "objective" to being "subjective" and from being a measurement to being a description and an analysis of a person's experience in a context.

This obviously poses difficulty for large poverty reduction interventions by the State, since increasingly now, these are confronted by the reality that increasing global poverty is a consequence of the exclusionary ways society creates and divides its resources. Poverty becomes the symptom of a larger systemic malaise, of institutional values that are given priority and the mechanisms and institutions that maintain these values. This viewpoint then necessitates transforming the structures and institutions within which the poor person lives, and not merely the life of the individual.

Although the World Bank's WDR and the Voices of the Poor (VOP) consultations have been much lauded, particularly for the latter's participatory process and its textured analyses of poverty, there are, nevertheless, two levels at which substantial critiques can been launched[5]. The first is methodological; the second is on the slippage en-route from the VOP to the WDR, specifically in the conceptualizations of two key aspects of poverty: redistribution and powerlessness.

At the methodological level, the critique stems from the caution about the instrumental and extractive uses of "participatory" methodology, and the types of knowledge that it creates and reproduces. Critics point out that these methodologies are "public events" that are still influenced by existing class and gender hierarchies (Mosse, 1994). Using a Foucauldian analysis, Cook, Kothari et. al (2001) point to the flawed assumptions[6] of participatory approaches that result in the re-inscription of local power structures, rather than challenging them. It can also lead to the reification of norms through surveillance and "consensus" building; and most importantly, it sanctifies the truth claims to the process of knowledge production: *"It 'purifies' knowledge and the spaces of participation through the codification, classification and control of information, and its analysis and (re)presentation* (Kothari, 2001:142).

Two key insights that emerged from the VOP were first, that redistribution has to form a part of the poverty reduction agenda. Second, it acknowledges that poverty is fundamentally a situation of powerlessness. However, though mentioned, both have been given inadequate theoretical attention in the WDR 2000. Furthermore, there is a "lag" between the World

Bank policy research (represented by the VOP and the WDR), and its translation into country lending practices (Mosley, 2001).

The powerlessness of the poor vis-à-vis institutions is central to the process of creating and sustaining poverty. Any serious attempt at poverty eradication has to grapple with the *processes* of powerful institutions, and the individuals that operate within them. A multi-dimensional view of poverty requires a multi-dimensional view of power and institutional responsibility (Chambers, 2001), at all levels. At a local level, it means taking seriously the VOP feedback from the poor that the police are the biggest impediment to their well-being. At an international level, it means questioning, as Chambers does, the reasons why the WDR uses obfuscatory language that conflates IFI loans with grants, or why it does not consider *debt avoidance* as an anti-poverty strategy:

"Debt avoidance is not considered or mentioned as a strategy. A clue to understanding this omission can be found in Box 7.10, which refers to 'Breaking the grip of money lenders...' and concluding that 'powerful vested interests can be expected to mobilize against reforms that seek to erode their position in the name of poor people...' We can ask: As moneylenders, are not the World Bank and the IMF powerful vested interests?" (Chambers, 2001)

A second critique, related to the previous, is regarding re-distribution. The WDR recognizes that high inequality is bad for economic growth, and therefore puts redistribution on the agenda. However, it retains conventional World Bank wisdom first, that trade liberalization will bring about re-distribution, and consequently, that inequality can change only slowly. Further, it advocates redistribution of assets that will avoid conflict (ruling out what it calls "populist" land reform measures, or raising progressive taxes), namely, improved public expenditure, particularly on education; and the participation of the poor". As White points out, these proposed measures for incremental redistribution are inadequate, because they do not take into account re-distribution within the financial system, nor do they seek means to ensure equitable distribution of the environmental, social, political capital (White, 2001).

The rather weak prescriptions on re-distribution are indicative of the WDR's emphasis on an instrumental *efficiency argument*, rather than a *human rights approach*.

"On the question of why redistribution matters: the WDR misses two important arguments which would strengthen the case. The first is about social inclusion, the second about rights. Both take the argument beyond the instrumental." (Maxwell, 2001)

A minimal agenda for re-distribution formulated by Maxwell first frames it within a *human rights paradigm,* as an essentially *political* project, which requires the creation of a culture of public accountability. The suggested measures include:

- Fiscal costing of the commitment to social protection
- Active, progressive tax policy; tax system used for re-distribution of assets
- Focus on rural development, since 60% of the world's 1.2 billion absolute poor are in rural areas, and will remain there on current trajectories till 2020
- Anti-discrimination policies
- Explicit govt policies to target poverty and inequality

New Directions: Social Exclusion and Human Rights paradigms

As the preceding overview of the theoretical approaches to poverty demonstrates, different national and international intellectual traditions have led to different policy emphases. Concepts are only as good as they way they are used, and drawing from the discussion above, this study would like to outline some premises for an anti-poverty framework and strategy this research study aims to articulate. Two key premises that under-gird this theoretical framework: First, that anti-poverty is a political project. The principles of social and economic justice inherent to a rights-based approach are therefore central, and take precedence over arguments of economic growth or efficiency. Second, taking forward the central concept of powerlessness, this study uses a social exclusion framework to articulate the role of institutions in creating and perpetuating poverty.

Social Exclusion is a concept that originated in French social theory, and has been deployed in recent theories of European welfare systems. A commonly cited definition of social exclusion is *'the processes through which individuals or groups are wholly or partially excluded from full participation in the society in which they live'* (European Foundation 1995:4). It is also a theoretical space to analyze behaviours that are degrading, contemptuous or disregarding that may have profound psychological effects. Silver (1994) outlines three paradigms of social exclusion that are operational in the North:

- Solidarity paradigm predominant in France, where the emphasis is on the rupture of the social bond, and the effort is towards social integration.
- Specialisation paradigm typical of the U.S, where the contractual exchange of rights and obligations within the liberal democratic framework are curtailed by discrimination, which results in un-enforced rights and market failures, leading to social exclusion.
- Monopoly paradigm current in the U.K and Northern Europe, emphasizes a Weberian view of social group monopolies constructed by coercive, hierarchical power relations and boundary closure.

Silver herself points out that these categorisations are heuristic devices, and are certainly not mutually exclusive. However, there are differences in definition, the central issues of exclusion (of whom, from what and how) and, consequently, policies. The arenas of social exclusion have been classified as: democratic and legal systems, markets, welfare state provisions and family/community; or more broadly as exclusion from Rights, Resources and Relationships (de Haan, 1998; 2007 & 2010).

Like the concept of social capital, social exclusion has permeated the development discourse in such a way that it means anything to anyone. Further, there is scepticism about the assumed superiority and applicability of Northern intellectual concepts to diverse developing country contexts (Rodgers et. al, 1997:5).

Despite these dangers of imprecision, there are two inherent characteristics of social exclusion that are significant and potentially useful for the discourse on poverty. The first is that it is a multi-dimensional concept that recognizes not only the economic, but also the political and social dimensions of deprivation. Second,

"...the concept *focuses on processes, and on the mechanisms and institutions* that exclude people. It may take us beyond static descriptions of situations of deprivation, and focus on the causes and mechanisms that lead to these situations.... In this, it also has policy relevance, since it identifies problems in existing institutions and options for improvement." (de Haan, 1998, our emphasis)

The first characteristic of multi-dimensionality brings the concept of social exclusion close to that of relative deprivation, and there is an area of overlap with vulnerability and capabilities approaches to poverty. It is the second characteristic, the focus on processes, which pushes towards recognition of institutional responsibility (Rodgers et. al, 1998), and therefore need for institutional, rather than individual change.

Defining and maintaining boundaries, defining rules and norms, decision-making, and determining resource allocation are some of the key processes through which exclusion is operationalized within institutions. Conversely, inclusion can occur through processes of integration (as in the French solidarity models), negotiation, and direct conflict.

The use social exclusion is a major point of departure for this study from the majority of other theoretical approaches to poverty. These approaches tend to avoid conceptualizing relationships of power, or if they do, may conceive of it as a static rather than a dynamic, iterative phenomenon. The framework used in this study also presumes the theoretical emphasis on processes and institutional accountability, without sacrificing the multi-dimensionality of the capability framework. The researcher has developed a template to understand institutional processes (of state, market, gender, caste, etc) in interaction with people's agency. Further, the researcher would like to apply the framework's underlying premise of institutional accountability to a scrutiny of the poverty process itself.

Evolving An Affirming Response To Poverty And Marginalisation

The human condition is deteriorating rapidly for many people because of the fragmentation of their traditional institutions, the indifference of the modern ones to human well-being, the destruction of nature and commons, and the failure of the nation state in its governance functions. As a result, more and more people are being impoverished and rendered dispensable, left to fend for their survival against insurmountable odds.

The urgency and scale with which the poor are being eradicated requires us to respond urgently. This action cannot be reactive and fragmented. Instead, this action must be holistic, and address systemic root causes of exploitation and exclusion. It must acknowledge the complex and intelligent nature of human and natural systems, their emergence and inter-relatedness. It must be committed to enabling an honest appraisal of the self and the context, revisiting intent, purpose and ethical standards. These standards have to be clear and steadfast. Guided by these ethical standards, action must aim to empower people and affirm their self-determination so as to enable their participation in public governance.

Even though the challenge faced seems insurmountable, in complex systems, solutions to current problems also lie embedded in this same system. There are several seeds of action that are emerging currently: restoration of current institutions, by rejuvenating traditional ones and humanising modern ones; formation of global and local collectivities, particularly people's movements in redressing justice and equity issues, and newly emergent peer networking and open source knowledge repositories based on horizontal networks rather than hierarchical structures. These potential systemic solutions are now being recognised and articulated.

To meet the challenge posed by impoverishing processes, there has to be a collective shift in a critical mass of people about the purpose of their institutions; when people are no longer evoked to act for limited self-gain, but also proactively act to critically determine public governance. Such critical citizen collectives may well be the pivot around which the cycle of poverty turns. For evolving such an affirming response it is very important that we learn from Gandhi. Particularly important is that we reformulate our understanding of poverty and marginalisation – abandon the expert understating and develop a grounds-up perspective that is tempered with people's own voices. A good starting point would be to begin it from Gandhi. In the following chapters we shall attempt that.

Conclusion

Poverty research is inevitably tied to the aspirations of policy making as they are concerned about propelling actions. But the last few decades of policy making and the actions resulting out of it, duly assisted by action research of the development studies, have compelled many of the sensitive ones among us to conclude that a lot of bad actions is much worse than no action at all. It was because the action research and the consequent actions were guided by much of self-serving notion and assumptions elaborated above in this chapter that in this research we aspire to avoid the pitfalls of conventional research.

End Notes

[1] The ratio of the income of the top percentile to the bottom percentile of the population, measured on a scale of 0-1.0. Figures closer to 1 represent higher levels of inequality.

[2] IFIs : International Financial Institutions - primarily refers to the World Bank, International Monetary Fund and the World Trade Organisation

[3] Poverty and Famines; Sen, pg 17, 1981

[4] For a comprehensive list of the targets, see: http://webnet1.oecd.org/pdf/M00017000/M00017310.pdf, and for the DAC Homepage, see: http://www1.oecd.org/dac/htm/pubsfoc.htm#DAC%20Policy%20Statements

[5] Other critiques offered are the lack of attention in WDR to key findings in the VOP about the importance of strategies of livelihoods promotion (rather than "job" creation); the diversity of the poorest; and the significance of the body as both an asset and a liability (Chambers, 2001).

[6] Some of these assumptions include the assumption of binary oppositions; the assumption that local knowledge is "fixed" rather than continuously constructed; the assumption that power is static, rather than discursive or circulatory.

II

Poverty Research: The (Middle) Road Not Taken

Introduction

Almost all poverty-specific research is principally conducted under the banner of Development Studies, whose origin can be traced back 1970s. Though Development Studies (it also includes policy studies) aspires to claim a place in the fold of social sciences, there is a crucial difference in their treatment of their respective objects of study, both in approach and in emphasis. For the former, poverty is a primary and avowed concern, whereas for the latter (particularly Sociology, Anthropology Political Science and Psychology) it is incidental that knowledge about poverty is added. Thus, the research model we wish to popularize has to clarify whether it brackets itself in the category of Development Research conducted in the fashion normalized by Development Studies discipline or in the category of a social science research. The difference between them is decisive, as some mutually challenging and reciprocally critical foundational notions guide them.

Choosing one over the other is not just a matter of research focus but also expressive of the values and worldview we stand by. Much of the research conducted under the umbrella of Development Studies in the form of poverty research tends to proceed by taking some crucial notions as given while Social science research would treat them as contestable and problematic. One can think of even "poverty" here. In the same way, the foundational conceptions of "society" and "human person" that underlay these two disciplines are different in a significant way. In a manner of saying, one might argue that social sciences have not dealt with poverty as exclusively as perhaps the Development Studies. The causes are political in both camps, despite the good that has happened in either of the camps. However, in the final analysis, poverty research not tempered by the debates and insights of the social sciences tends to produce conclusions and results that are incomplete and superficial, when not self-serving.

In the remaining pages I comment on the overall spirit of the development research, obliquely, by discussing the general tendencies in poverty research and my criticisms of them. I will also dwell upon the problems of social sciences vis-à-vis their concerns with poverty.

The comments are organised around the following questions:

1. Why social sciences particularly Sociology, Anthropology Political Science and Psychology – do not concern themselves with poverty exclusively and what are the lessons we can take from them?
2. What are the problems of conceptualizing poverty in poverty research and how development research can do away with them?
3. If social sciences have any thing to say about poverty, then what can they be and how they are relevant to development research?

Poverty and Destitution

The biggest problem of studies about poverty is that there is poverty of studies about issues of poverty in sociology. But in reality "Poverty was never a problem but destitution was"[1] writes Asish Nandy. The pre-modern societies or even pre-modern minded in the modern societies, did not regard poverty as a problem. It exists sometimes as a voluntary renunciation of worldly pleasures or as the outcome of karma, or as a punishment for too much boasting or ill-will for others. It never meant starving or abandonment. The person in poverty had clothes, food and shelter, perhaps lesser in quality or quantity than what was normal for the wider society. But he had them. Starvation death and famine are modern inventions as Amartya Sen would have us convinced. It is worth quoting Nandy further on this;

Poverty is not destitution. When some intellectuals and activists talk of poverty being degrading or reject any critique of development as romanticization of poverty, they actually have in mind destitution, not poverty, but are too clever by half to admit that. By collating or collapsing these two terms, apologists of development have redefined all low-consuming, environment-friendly lifestyles as poor and, thus, degrading and unfit for survival in the contemporary world... Destitution, or at least large-scale destitution, is a more recent phenomenon. It has been increasing among many traditionally poor communities over the last hundred years, partly as a direct result of urbanization and development. The most glaring instances of destitution are found not in traditional, isolated tribal communities, but among the poor communities that are uprooted and fragmented and move into cities as individuals or nuclear families. It is also found among landless agricultural laborers who for some reason lose their jobs in a situation where agriculture is industrialized or becomes nonprofitable. They are the ones who find themselves unable to cope with the demands of an impersonal market or the culture of a modern political economy. Indeed, when we talk of poverty, we usually have that other kind of created poverty in mind, but are too defensive to admit that. We suspect that our world-views, ideologies and lifestyles are in league with the creation of this new kind of modern poverty[2].

Poverty as an integral part of social existence, but not as the opposite of wealth or richness has got transmorphed into a stain or shame, only thanks to the sleight of hand of modernity and the disciplines that it spawned.

It all happened in 1949 January 10, when Harry Truman declared nearly two billion people and the most nations of southern hemisphere as underdeveloped or poor. Before this the peoples of Asia, Africa and Latin America did not always see themselves in terms of "poverty." This is relatively recent; it goes back only as far as the early post-World War II period, when the apparatuses of knowledge production and intervention (the World Bank, the United Nations, bilateral development agencies, planning offices in the Third World, etc.) were established and when a whole new political economy of truth - different from that of the colonial or pre-war period - was set into place. None would have predicted that this qualification would become part of the self-image of the people in these nations. It unleashed such a sudden sense of shame and self-disparagement in the psyches of these nations and the people in them, that removing this became the avowed mission of every nation, elites, international agencies and governments.

They have more or less successfully transferred this self-definition onto their non-cash earning, non-monetized asset possessing people who never thought that they were ever poor. In this, the entire army of international development experts, agencies and national elites and bureaucrats joined hands to declare first the nations as poor then the vast sections of the people in them. Thus poverty became shame - national and personal shame at that. Now, poverty as shame tends to generate self-images in the countries and people in them that treat poverty as problematic to be immediately dealt with and instantly banished. "Normal" middle class citizens, particularly those belonging to the liberal-democratic tradition, are uncomfortable with these paradoxes. They usually push them under the carpet through various psychological subterfuges. Who wants to live in moral discomfort when easy escapes are available in the form of popular ideologies of development?" For them poverty assumes a life of its own as a ghost that must be exorcised. It is not caused by those who wish to banish it. It is something that exists before. As Maia Green explains, "Poverty is ascribed agency to impact on the lives of people who `fall into' it. Poverty is not described as a consequence of social relations, but represented as an evolving entity that must be `attacked'. Size matters. The growth in poverty, its sheer scale, prompts a response. Poverty in these development writings is represented as inherently problematic, not only for the poor themselves, whose suffering is graphically documented, but for the wider society which is threatened by it."[3]

But what was getting defined as poverty was lack of money or lack of absorption of certain amount calories. This has sidestepped that which produced real shame, namely, destitution and kept itself busy with something that can be managed technocratically and bureaucratically, because it has been de-contextualized, universalized and quantified. It was contented that this disembodied disease called poverty can be eradicated and managed only with modern institutional apparatuses. It is important to be sensitive to the resonances of disease metaphor. Just as disease management and control became the means to define diseases and normalize modern institutions and the attitudes consistent with them, poverty management institutionalizes modernity through privileging of an array of institutions and an army of experts. If the spread and ferocity of disease say like cholera were attributed to the 'potentially threatening' behavior of the poor who steeped as they are in traditions, poverty too was traced to the non-internalization or non-intrusion of modern outlook and attitudes in the poor. Hence the study of poverty becomes the study of poor. With poverty as a subject the poor, who by definition lack the resources and entitlements to reframe the terms of this engagement, become objects of study.

It is one thing to internalize the ethos of modern labour and all other concomitant value frameworks associated with it, and it is another thing to accept the intruding power of the experts. They derive their intrusion rights in the form of grand narratives such as 'Industrialization", "family planning", the "Green Revolution," "macroeconomic policy", "integrated rural development" and the like. These become the conduits for radically reorganizing the lives of the wider society in the image of modern societies who have supposedly banished the disease of poverty. They repeats the same basic 'truth', namely, that permitting their interventions is paving the way for the achievement of those conditions that characterize rich societies: industrialization, agricultural modernization, and urbanization. In this process poverty itself is regarded as the vestige of pre-modern societies and truly modern person cannot and need not be poor.

Poverty as not-modern

The logic of modernity by aligning with the discourses on poverty tends to produce a definition of poverty as something that is non-modern. 'Modern Man' may not be the richest, but he is definitely not poor, even in the economic sense. If someone is poor, it is because of his personal inadequacy to absorb the virtues of modernity and its ethos[4]. As Max Weber would argue, poverty under conditions of capitalism, with protestant ethics having modernized itself, would only mean that if someone is starving for want of money, he or she has not acquired the capitalist spirit, which is very much a product of modernity. Bauman affirms this association in a different way, by explaining the perennial concern of the modern societies and state about poor and poverty as an attempt at converting the lazy poor into productive labourers, who would learn to work in the factories by absorbing modern work ethics. He further adds strength to the thesis that poor person is non-modern, by tracing the sudden elision of poor from the discourses of development in the developed world to an assessment normalized in these societies' that poor are not important anymore as they have not internalized the virtues of consumption and also do not posses resources to participate in consumerist culture. The post-modern societies do not need the poor any more. The indispensability of the poor is an abandoned idea. Now societies can do without poor. But that is a story for the west. The east still needs poor! Not only that, it is only in the name of the poor, it can even continue its modernizing and self-serving missions. Historically informed perspectives on poverty reveal not only the social construction of the category within specific historical and institutional settings, and the key role of powerful institutions in globalising the poverty agenda, but also the fact that the constitution of the kind of poverty that development practitioners aspire to reduce is itself a product of the socio economic relations of modernity.

At another level being poor is equated with being non-modern, is in the way poor were disciplined in hard labour. This equation is as old as industrialization itself. Poor are poor because they have not internalized the virtues of industrialism, an unmistakable modern product. They were the basis of discourses about poverty and social responsibility for the destitute in England until the mid twentieth century, hence the intentionally punitive welfare regimes in workhouses where the destitute could go to seek food and shelter in return for hard labour in conditions that were explicitly designed to replicate the prison. Related attitudes live on in popular perceptions of poverty even within poor communities (Woodhouse 2003) and within the international development community. The latter's food for work programme and other food-aid in place of direct cash as relief is predicated on the assumption that the poor should learn to earn his/her food through hard labour, thereby learning the virtues of modern industrial society.

All these lead to the dichotomous and dualistic construction of the poor as reified category and further imputation of same solidity to a society of the poor, as if there is such a reality existing, and the simultaneous construction of non-poor universe consisting of the experts who study poverty and the poor[5]. The world of non-poor appropriates the right to criticize and alter the lives and universe of the poor. As has been forcefully argued by Yapa, "Dualistic thinking pervades the entire notion of a poverty sector which is viewed as a distinct, measurable, bounded entity, that part of the economy where the poor reside - the locus of the poverty problem; those who are not poor reside in the realm of the non-problem. The poverty sector has little capital and no resources. Presumably that is why it is poor. Capital, technology and resources must be infused from outside. The sector of the non-poor is the seat of intellect, resources and solutions - the knowing subject reflecting on the problems of the needy object, an idea well- captured in the term 'poor as target group"[6]. Crucially, the criticism against poor tends to get further leveled against the society of the poor, there by exonerating the wider society from the crime of creating poverty in the first place. With this, not only the incommensurability of worlds of the poor and the world of the non-poor becomes firmly established but also the right of the world of the non-poor to intervene into the world of the poor. The victors now have no ear for the losers. The emphasis on poverty as the problem and the locus of analysis diverts attention from the social relations, local, national and international, which produce poverty as an attribute of people.

But the experts and their disciplines would not problematise the role of the world-outside-poor, both at the national and international levels, as the reasons for spewing poverty in the lives of the poor. But either would ignore or reify poverty as if it resides in the world of poor caused by endogenous factors specific to the society of the poor. This has led to a paradoxical situation of complete neglect of or excessive obsession with poverty. While the act of ignoring has been adopted by social sciences such as sociology and social anthropology, the act of attributing poverty to endogenous factors has been the stance of development studies. Within the realm of social science practices, once poverty has been conceived as caused by factors immanent in the society of the poor, in the name of 'Culture of Poverty' debate for example, poor are left on their own and focus get shifted onto wider social system of whose abnormality is poverty. Hence poverty occupies least space in the consciousness of the social scientists, even while it assumes enormous importance in the minds of state and NGO sector, aided as they were by Development Studies, for they seek to legitimize modernization processes and thereby their own centrality in heralding them in post-independent India.At another level, what has been the omission of social sciences has become the reason for development studies' engagement with poverty and poor as social category, thereby creating a rationale for imposition of modernity. It needs a bit more elaboration.

Poverty Studies and Social sciences

Poverty studies in all their manifestations within the Development Studies fold, are seemingly immune to the critical inputs from social sciences. Pitching their significance only in relation to policy influencing and policy making, they sacrifice research rigour and critical inquiry for the sake of arriving at spectacularly grand generalizations that are amenable to policy formulations. In the same spirit, seldom do they engage in a self-reflexive inquiry into their own ways of constructing the categories that are now taken as 'given', for example 'poverty' as a construct. Since their very existence and relevance rest on postulating a foundational reality called 'poverty', they present it as a well-rounded singular object and as an ever-persisting reality. The kind of alternative research that I suggest should therefore be sensitive to this lacuna in poverty studies. Even though it is not our primary purpose in our endeavour here to elaborate on the benefits of reflexive exercise in the research we are proposing, we should remain tempered by the spirit of reflexive inquiry through out our altenative research exercise.

In the following pages I seek to hightlight the idea of seizing upon the opportunity to bring in the insights offered by social sciences, particularly anthropology. Because, it is only in the light of anthropology, we realize that poverty studies have never benefited from an intense ethnographic research on the poverty experiences of individuals. Actually much of the participatory approaches within Development Studies are short-term engagement with acquiring people's perception on poverty. Hence, it is incumbent upon development research to complement the survey-based and PRA-based poverty research with ethnographic research. This not only has high degree of intellectual value but also political value, since the latter concerns the politics of poverty research. The inferences we can make from anthropological ethnographic research tell us many striking things about what is absent and what is overly present in poverty studies, though it may be instructive to remember that Social sciences including anthropology are not *overtly* concerned about poverty, for reasons delineated below. Therefore, asking poverty studies to behave like social sciences is not only overambitious, but even questionable. However, there are certain tendencies in social sciences that have to be emulated in poverty studies as much as there are certain practices and conceptual shortcuts in poverty studies that have to be abandoned. Indeed, the problems of poverty studies become more glaring only in the light of the spirit of reflexivity that so wonderfully characterizes social sciences. Thus, we are going to benefit immensely by knowing why poverty is not studied by social sciences with the same intensity as poverty studies, as much as by the awareness as to why poverty studies do it obsessively.

The Poverty-Focus or the Lack of It in Social sciences

In what follows, let us try to grapple with the question of why poverty was not the proclaimed object of study for mainstream social science disciplines such anthropology, sociology, political science and psuchology. There are two kinds of reasons on may attribute:

1. Those concerning the inherent politics and methodological rigidities of social sciences and
2. The politics intrinsic to conceptualizing poverty itself.

Historical Legacies

The first kind of reasons flows from the historical and methodological legacies of social sciences. Historically, social sciences were born in times when the western hegemony was establishing itself through colonialism very stridently. As the products of modernity these disciplines mostly sided with the colonial empires and furthered their agendas. Though there were dissenting voices within social science fold, the dominant voices were supportive of the colonizing forces as they saw the latter as the harbingers of modernity. Though the criminal intentions of the colonizing forces were taken note of by the most conscientious among the social scientists, they were pardoned, for they were treated as necessary costs to be paid for promoting and disseminating modernity. In this sense, the social scientists were willingly missing the trees of criminal acts of colonialism for the wood of modernizing intentions of the imperial forces.

Thus, the social sciences were more focused at the processes that contributed to the dissemination and effects of modernity. As a result, poverty was treated as the reality specific only to the non-modern societies, and poverty was regarded as the manifestation of the deadweight of the traditions. Hence social science research was obsessively fixated with modernity and the factors that promote it. If caste, race, agrarian economy, village power relations etc were studied by Social Sciences it was not so much for the impoverishment they caused but for the challenges they posed for the spread of modernity. Poverty and other social ills were thought to melt into air with the arrival of modernity. The untrammeled optimism for modernity and the redemptions it will bring upon the societies mired in traditions had persuaded the social scientists to give scant attention to poverty. If any thing, poverty was regarded as a problem coming in the way of modernity marching successfully. By strengthening modernity, poverty was thought to disappear.

Methodological Rigidities

Secondly, on the methodological front too there was least encouragement for grappling with poverty, let alone conceptualizing it. Much of social science disciplines particularly sociology, political sciences, and anthropology, were steeped in functionalist and systemic paradigm, due to which they were intensely concerned about normal state of affairs in the society and about the processes and means for maintaining it. Poverty and all its manifestations were regarded as abnormal and therefore dysfunctional to the society. While the social scientist was alarmed at the higher incidences of abnormality in society, they still treated them as the excreta that would be washed away by the oncoming waves of normalcy achieved by the engulfment of the entire society by modernity. The social scientists' persuasive recommendations for social engineering were aimed at working on the reinstatement of normalcy. It was believed that normalcy defined in modernist spirit will establish the equilibrium and will banish abnormality in theirs wake. This resulted in the whole focus centering on social engineering and the effects of it on the wider society.

Poverty thus was consigned to the status of the crust on the surface of the society that will have to be eliminated forthwith through social engineering efforts. Social sciences, as they were growing in the shadow of the supremacy of scientific rigour in natural sciences, had assigned the task of studying poverty to less theoretical disciplines like social work and development studies. However, the latter were 20th century phenomena and very much the product of the social engineering orientation of the social sciences. While Social Work has come as an answer to the concern of the mainstream society to integrate many 'marginal' (read, deviant) groups into mainstream modernity, Development Studies aspired to objectify poverty so that doing so would help development professionals and the agencies they belong to have a "problem" that can be "managed". The results: social work located the problem of marginalization and impoverishment in the groups that were marginalized, rather than in the forces that marginalized them in the first place. Development studies, on the other hand, solidified the multifaceted experience of impoverishment into a managerial issue for the development sector. Impoverished persons too were understood in the same sense. Poor are persons who failed to integrate themselves into the redeeming processes of modernity, for reasons mostly personal – personal incapacity, inability and inadequacy. Many of the development studies disciplines in various incarnations too took this up uncritically and went about understanding, assessing and measuring poverty without ever problematising it as a relational product. Poverty was understood by the Development Studies only with a biomedical perspective, which treated poverty as a disease that has crept into society like a germ into the human body. It was in the manner of going to war that poverty was approached.

The Concern with Processes

It does not however mean that social sciences were not concerned with poverty. Social sciences too studied poverty in the sense of grappling with the experiences and various ways of coping with it. This was happening, even while social sciences grew out of their modernity fixations, crossed on to post-modern territories and became critical of social engineering as such.

The post-colonial period saw social sciences becoming characterised by their reflexivity about their own practices and the politics they had normalized. This brought to light how social sciences were engaged as pamphleteers for modernity and in the process invented the backwardness of non-modern societies. This brought the curtain down on even the peripheral possibility of studying poverty per se, as it was the invention of a modern mind to suit and privilege the colonizing intentions. And also as ever, with the primary concern centering on understanding social, political and cultural processes, social sciences virtually had ceased to engage with creating an object called poverty that could be measured and grasped tangibly. If anything, they only became critical of such objectification of poverty. Their interest in processes led them to study how social actors deal with and become part of social processes. Simultaneously, another camp within social sciences was engaged in studying the institutions and structures that sustain and maintain the social processes. Accordingly, in social sciences the understanding of poverty begins from the processes and leads to people who are impacted by these processes. This is the inverse of what transpires in development studies in which such understanding proceeds from and ends with the poor and what happens to them.

Curiously, despite the dearth of exclusive attention paid to poverty per se, much of the alternative conceptions of poverty have come from social sciences. Particularly the contribution of anthropology in highlighting alternative conceptions of poverty is immense. It has to be remembered, however, that anthropology was the handmaiden of colonial forces throughout the period, when imperial forces were riding roughshod over many third world societies. However, in their concern with understanding the cultures of many third world societies, they brought to limelight many new ways and perspectives of experiences of poverty. More significantly their contribution towards the cross-cultural understanding of poverty and the differential experiences of poverty in different cultural settings is immensly valuable.

Therefore, various categories of people identified to be among the poorest population, such as disabled, widows, beggars etc were not studied in the same way as development disciplines studied them. For the latter it was a 'given' that they are poor because their life circumstances fit into models already developed to identify poor persons. But in the case of social sciences what is more important are the social processes that operate in relation to them. In that sense these groups of population are as significant for study as the groups which the development studies would have qualified as non-poor. Moreover, for social sciences, the development studies' cardinal division of the population into poor and non-poor is immaterial as they are interested in the interaction among social actors in the generic sense of the term.

Development as Elimination of Poverty

The absence of poverty discourses in social sciences can also be explained in terms of how they conceptualize development. Development in social sciences is understood in mostly positive terms, in that it was treated in terms of several *presences* that affirmed development. For example, development was measured in terms of what has to be established rather than in terms of what has to be eliminated. A society was regarded as developed if it has acquired scientific spirit, rational attitude and economic prosperity. It was believed that the establishment of these traits would drive away all other problems and social ills. With this understanding, social sciences had taken upon themselves the task of informing various social forces as to how these presences can be brought in. Such conception of development compelled them to study those processes that maintain or facilitate or act as impediments to these traits. Most of the social sciences' energies were spent on the functional aspects and other equilibrium-maintaining processes. Sadly, those absences and dysfunctional elements were treated with contempt and were thought to disappear in the face of modernizing forces.

However, the heightened attention given to poverty in international development studies had a lot to do again with their conception of development. In their conception, development was understood in terms of the elimination of negative presences. Development is such a state in society when poverty and other such 'social ills' are eliminated. In development studies' perspective, poverty and other such phenomena were given the kind of place that disease occupied in biomedical disciplines. Therefore, maintenance of normalcy calls for singling out the disease and bringing it under the microscope for analysis, measurement and management. Poverty was a disease and it was studied in the same spirit in which diseases were studied in medical sciences. For these disciplines, development is the 'normal' state that every society has to strive for. However, now there is an easy way out to achieve development (easy way out only *conceptually* but not in reality where poverty elimination proves to be an elusive task) – eliminate poverty and there comes development! The easy equivalence of development with the absence of poverty triggered off unfettered interest in poverty, its kinds and types.

This explains why social development knowledge is all about poverty. Yet the generation of such knowledge has an instrumental purpose. The politics of such equivalence between development and elimination of poverty will be elaborated later. However, it suffices here to say that the arrival of international development studies has a lot to do with sudden concern with poverty in the last five decades. It all began with the World Bank becoming actively engaged in poverty eradication after few decades of wishful thinking that economic growth leads to the elimination of social ills like poverty. The linkage of this knowledge to management-of-poverty-anxiety is quite evident in the way many development organisations and state agencies use them for control and evolving interventions strategies. The proliferation of knowledge about poverty soon reached its crescendo with the institutionalisation of Development Studies across the globe, promoted and sponsored by international finance organisations, among other big forces. What was missing in Development Studies discipline was the kind of reflexivity that became so crucial for social sciences. Hence the politics of studying poverty never came to light until social scientists probed into it. The next section will deal with it.

The Politics of Understanding Poverty

Poverty became an issue of grave importance only in the last three decades. Ever since human and social development was no longer assumed to be an automatic concomitant of economic development and as something that had to be actively pursued and established, social development has become a big techno-managerial concern of the development agencies, both that of the state and non-state. This shift has bred a different understanding of poverty and who the poor are. This shift has also legitimized the arrival and continued presence of an army of development institutions, organisations and professionals that have assumed the mandate of facilitating, achieving and consolidating development in the societies and groups deemed underdeveloped *by them*. They have all come together to create a particular reality called poverty in a fashion that validates their interventions in the society and the lives of the impoverished members in it. The way, in which international development organisations, particularly World Bank, have suddenly brought poverty at centre of the development discourse, hides certain self-serving intentions of these institutions, rather than just the noble concerns for the poor. At once, poverty was very extensively and vigorously studied by Development Studies. Many poverty studies soon ensued. In the long run, both the noble and not-so-noble intentions of poverty studies have conspired and worked overtime to establish a distinct ontological reality of being poor and poverty. It is as if they have carved out a new species of human – the one who is in poverty. Presently let us examine a series of assumptions that have acquired axiomatic proportions in Development research and have gone great length to invest species-specific qualities in poor, as it were.

Convenient Assumptions

Insinuating the inevitability of Development Interventions

One such convenient assumption is that persons in poverty cannot cope with poverty without the support of the development sector, be it the state or NGOs. These Development actors justify their interventions into the lives of the persons in poverty without taking into account those people's abilities of self-help and coping. Development studies and even practices conveniently gloss over the truth that the poor have always coped with poverty and survived it in history. If anything, it is only with the arrival many of those very forces that seek to remove poverty in lives of the poor, that poverty has become an unmanageable challenge in the lives of the poor to a large extent. That is why in many of the anthropological research undertaken in Africa we find that the essential component of the actions that the poor undertake to deal with poverty involves moving beyond the perimeters of the circles within which both the state and development organisations operate and influence. Even in Indian contexts a sensitive researcher may discover the desire of those being poor to evaluate their capabilities to deal with poverty outside the support, parameters and definitions provided by the development actors of both the state and non-state variety. In other words, modern forces, including the development actors such as the state and development organisations of all varieties, have incapacitated the poor not only by what they omitted to do, but also by what they committed to do.

This is true even in those individuals, categories of populations and communities that have decided to selectively relate to the state and development organisations. In their poverty-confronting efforts of the poor, there are many situations that do not have any scope for the involvement of either the state or the development organisations. It may thus be said that, in many aspects of the lives of those being the poorest, the development actors may not have any relevance at all, or at best only a marginal presence. It should awaken the development personnel from their delusions that poverty cannot be eradicated without their active support, involvement and presence. As a matter of fact, in specific situations, the poor are well served by the development sector when they do not serve them at all. This is because these development actors bring in their train a whole lot of value system, moral frameworks and cultural scales (in this context, they are that of modern or other dominant paradigms such as Brahminical Hindutva) that not only define them as poor or the poorest before commencing their poverty-elimination work, but also by a stroke of definition and conceptual jugglery, push them to the peripheries by locating the centres in some other places other than the ones that are the native to the people they choose to work with.

It is exactly for these reasons that development is conceived of by some sensitive minds, not as the product of the expansion and influence of development sector, but by banishing their influence from the respective territories. Gandhian vision is one such alternative conception of development that visualizes the return of self-worth and self-sufficiency in the people the moment they abandon the civilizational attributes of modern western societies.

It is a matter for lengthy debate whether development research has been sensitive to the above accusation. But if one considers even the attempts by it to document the self-supporting and coping abilities of the poor, one notices it having serious problems that nullify such sensitivity they may have had to the criticism above. What are the problems of development research's understanding of people's abilities of self-help? We will consider them below.

The Skewed Concerns of PRA Approaches with Human Agency

When participatory approaches do take note of these indigenous strategies of coping with difficult situations, in the absence of a long-term ethnographic research, they fail to comprehensively stand by and incorporate the highly inventive coping abilities of those in poverty. Even if they were captured by the PRA or PPA processes, they have been removed from the people's living contexts, and blindly accorded heroic status or, at worst, condemned as inconsequential.

Even the most sympathetic and sensitive of the studies documenting the coping strategies of the persons in poverty and aspiring to evolve grounds-up perspectives of poverty has kept a very narrow operational definition for understanding human agency. These studies, in their drive to capture the indigenous strategies of the poor in dealing with poverty, split the social creativity of the poor into discrete behaviours and dispositions, and romanticize them as extraordinary feats, to say the least. There is this danger of predicating such creative responses of the poor on a highly individual and rationalist paradigm, and explain them away in terms of the means-end relationship.

There is another greater risk of validating the social creativity of the people-in-poverty in terms of the needs it fulfills, both for the poor who deploy theses strategies and for the development sectors that have an easy way out of the top-heavy and expertise-dependency accusations leveled at them. These need-based explanations of creativity are grossly unfair to the essential genius of the humans, leave alone the one who are being poor. People do not express creativity and engage in creative endeavours in order to fulfill certain constitutional needs of their body, nor even psyche. The mobilization of creative energies in humans happens as a matter of natural responses of living life as humans. In other words, expression of creativity is not like the work we engage for survival. The latter happens in response to the need to sustain oneself, whereas the former is an integral aspect of living.

To say that poor tribals in Africa take part in carnivals as a response to the lack of grandiosity in their normal regular life, is to say that the intensity with which they express their creativity in carnival is directly proportionate to the intensity of meaninglessness in real life. This is as unfair to the poor who would continue to take part in the carnivals even after getting out of poverty, as it is to the non-poor who, as humans, express creativity in these carnivals as an organic response. In a similar vein, to cite one example, the film-viewing behaviours of the poor in India cannot be explained away in terms of the lack of meaning and grandiosity in real life, against the drabness of which film is said to offer fantasy as an escape.

This is what happens even in highly sensitive pro-poor studies. They abstract singular behavioural traits of the poor out of the larger social process spanning across both time and space, and pit them against the immediate personal and even spiritual needs allegedly felt by the poor persons. This sort of positing cause and effect relationship fails to invest the poor with the energy, curiosity and right to deal with broader social challenges, other than poverty. One of the most unfair and gross reduction that has happened (and continues to happen) in much of the poverty research is to depict poor as perennially engaged with poverty alone in life, as if they are not actively and creatively engaged in confronting challenges other than that which concerns their mere bodily survival. As elaborated below, for many individuals characterized as poor, being poor it is just one among many social positions they occupy, though mostly as a compulsion. Similarly dealing with bodily survival – what would otherwise be named poverty, is just one among many of the challenges facing those being poor now.

This is here that the absence of ethnographic insights into the lives of the poor becomes glaringly conspicuous. The few such unintended-to-study-poverty anthropological studies rescue poor from their dealing-with-poverty obsession, into which development research has fixed them forever. The ethnographic research confirms that, just like the non-poor, poor are also engaged in negotiations with other challenges that range from constructing their own forms of modernity, to defining their own place in globalisation and national culture at the macro level, as well as earning for their own significance in their kin-network and concerning with question of power in their communities at the micro-levels. All these are beyond the issues of poverty and survival.

The Singular Social Identity of the Poor

Another crucial self-serving assumption that poverty studies have valorized in the discourses of poverty is the singular social identity for the poor. Indeed, the cursory perusal of many poverty studies points to the way they have variously confirmed, very unfairly, that for the persons they have studied, being poor is the only social identity. By fixing and freezing the impoverished people in the identity of poor, through its deployment of externally evolved indices, poverty research has served its personal interest well, even while obviating other social identities which people move into and out from. It is exactly because of this congealment of individual identities in their beings as poor, poverty studies have largely lost sight of the processual aspects of both poverty and being poor.

Ethnographic research of various varieties in anthropology confirms the fact that being poor is one among the many social identities people posses. And it is not that on all occasions they call themselves poor, even when the external variables evolved by development professional would label them so almost oppressively. Many such policy formulations also aim at trapping them in their poor status across all times and space. In contrast, one is often struck by the interest and concern of the people in poverty to deal with many other things in life, other than just poverty. This was, notwithstanding development professionals obsessively relapsing into asking poverty-specific questions, when doing poverty research. Those persons interviewed in such situations were aspiring to represent themselves as being equally, if not more, concerned about other challenges in life, than about poverty alone.

The Plea for Different Ontological Conception of Human Person

The arguments should not be construed to mean that development research should not be aimed at studying poverty at all. Far from it, such efforts should take into account the processes that *trap* as well as *free* people from fixed social locations. This will also help us to move towards those sections of population which do not have the luxury of even such fluidity, and gets fixed in such poor status forever even by their own definitions. Nevertheless, we have to be very cautious in positing such idea of person with singular identity, for the sociological wisdom warns us that social actors can never be trapped into a singular identity consistently as they always move from one social region to another, while assuming varying identities as they move through. Thus, our understanding of the poor and poverty can benefit from the qualification we have mentioned above. This would boil down to mean that the poorest person would be one who continues to treat oneself as being poor despite moving across different social regions or, even worse, would not be able to move into different regions at all, other than the one that locates that person as poor in the given moment.

Therefore, firstly, our commitment to treat people as an end in themselves and not as a means for enhancing economic productivity should be based on our vision to see 'being poor' as one of the many ways of being persons by the people we work with. Such commitment behooves us to move beyond the much-vaunted conceptualization of poverty as multidimensional experience and phenomenon. We should proceed to the multidimensional nature of poverty, from the decisive premise that being a person in society is a multidimensional experience, within which being poor is an experience that certain individuals undergo recurringly. Our focus ought to be on these individuals who by their own definitions move into and occupy the identity of poor more often than others and more permanently than others.

Secondly such commitment should also be informed by the learning that the multidimensional aspects of poverty are socially embedded in relationships and processes. Therefore, locating poverty experiences and poverty processes in the terrain of social relationship is supremely essential. Therefore, a proper analysis of the social relationship and social processes assumes importance. Sadly most of the participatory approaches have failed to capture the relational and processual aspects of being poor, for even the longest of the PRA or PPA exercises, is short when measured by ethnographic research standards. The latter guide us to focus on social processes and patterns of social relations that constitute an individual experiences and sense of identity.

Poor are not in Groups?

In the same breadth one has to critically reflect on the practice of poverty studies to categorize people into groups that are labeled as poor. For example, the classic understanding of disabled, homeless, widows, beggars, street children and other as groups of poor population is, in true sociological sense, problematic and even questionable. For one thing, they do not share the essential characteristic of groups or communities, as, apart from that which we attribute to them, they do not necessarily have common experiences specific to being disabled, street children, homeless etc. If, anything many of the attributes are applicable to all these groups. Such groupings tend also to gloss over their socially embedded experiences of being poor, as well as their singular strategies to deal with that identity of being poor. For example, in the case of the disabled and elderly, that person's experiences of poverty is not so much to do with being elderly and disabled but rather to do with whether or not s/he has family members or other forms of social support to turn to. Thus, there is a great deal of variability as to how the persons being poor use the social relationship and make meanings out of the social processes. This may be common between ones classified as poor with that of other ones from another category, and not necessarily common with another person like him/her.

We are not arguing that these classifications are not important, but they must be treated as such, and not attributed an uncritical commonality, thereby flattening the multiplicity of experiences of being the same type of poor, as arising out of differing relational contexts occupied by them. The danger is by reifying these classifications, a whole array of development efforts and policymaking are made that eventually end up causing more distress than they seek to eliminate. It is instructive to remember that much more than poverty, it is the solutions to get out of poverty that have proved problematic to people.

Poor and Institutional Reflections

The running thread throughout this study is the centrality accorded to human person – her experiences, and perceptions. Since the impact of poverty acquires salience on individual body and soul, there is specific emphasis on the effects of poverty on the human person and the human body. However the way out of poverty calls for collective efforts, therefore the focus on the agency of the individuals who can collectively herald situations that enhance fullest realisation of their human agency. Full play and assertion of human agency which can create and control situations where the creative unfolding of all human capabilities can occur is the prerequisite for redemption from the poverty-creating processes and poverty-sustaining institutions. This is not an individual achievement alone. A whole array of actors, including the poor themselves, has to collectively work towards bringing about such conditions.

This is corroborated in the findings of the study where the poor repeatedly reaffirm their commitment to living with dignity, apart essentially from having the basic necessities met. When having to resort to immoral or sub-human means of survival, what continues to hurt the poor is the lack of dignity, not just lack of food and other essentials alone. This is even by their own standards, not by the standards of middle class morality that tends to go one step further and criminalise their life choices. Hence even the ones, who make reasonable amount of money to meet their basic needs more than adequately, still regard themselves as severely impoverished, namely beggars and sex workers. This is because of the compulsion to live a body-dependent existence where they are seen only as working bodies without any of the attributes of human life accorded to them. That is why there is this perennial attempt by the sex worker to see her as a wholesome person, expressed in the form of her choosing to live as a wife and beget children, as any other 'normal' women, against being treated as an object of consumption by the clients. Her choice is made even if it means having to live with inadequate money and resources.

It is clear therefore that the poor detests being reduced to a cog in the production process and consequently being reduced to their bodies. In the face of such reduction as well as simultaneous criminalisation on the one hand and unable to change the prevailing production relations and institutional arrangements on the other hand, the poor feel compelled to take recourse to two choices. One is that they let the 'work' enter into their bodies—become sex workers or bonded labourers. The other is to give up their dependents—whom they are bound to nurture (if children) or support (if elderly) and protect—to the ever-demanding struggle for survival. This leads to child labour, elderly people working till they literally drop dead, women forced to work outside the home in addition to all the work within. When even these forms of poverty become acute, poverty is inherited through generations. Debt is worked off through generations.

By the time the poor become the 'absolute' poor, they lose any semblance of humanity in the eyes of the formal and informal institutions. They are referred to by the name of their tools of work. They are bought and sold like cattle to the slaughter. They can be—and are—separated from their families at will. Their right to conjugal life is on the same plane as the animals cruelly separated at birth and joined for mating only to produce more labouring bodies.

Even in the midst of all these debilitating effect of impoverishing processes, one is struck by the aliveness and continuous exercising of human agency of the poor. Their strategies of organising meaningful social universes are many and immensely creative, albeit their inability to bring about structural transformation leading to a just and equitable social order. This is because they are discrete individual acts of coping and meaning-making. In fact the constant debate over whether moving out of poverty is an individual or a collective effort is addressed by the poor themselves—and the conclusions are startling. The poor themselves need agency—the power to act—individually. But it is only by acting in concert with others that they can definitively make a difference. The stories all narrate individual attempts at coping. To move out of poverty, such effort is clearly not enough. Indeed, even coping at the present levels of acute poverty is possible only by the collective effort of the entire family. This is because the poor are operating under conditions and relations beyond their control. Their immediate demand is for a sensitive response from the wider society which does not criminalise their life-affirming strategies. From all other set of actors who have been vested with responsibilities, either voluntarily or contractually, to create better world, they expect recognition of their agency, rights and absolute solidarity for expanding choices for a dignified living.

This translates into looking at poverty from the perspective of the poor, and then at the process of moving out of poverty as a task to be determined at the pace and capacity of the poor themselves. It becomes clear that the person living in poverty has to be freed from the compulsions of exchanging her body. Only when her existence is the function of creative use of mind in wholesome union with body, and there is possibility for sustained investment in the progressive unfolding of capabilities in humans, can well–being result. Once the poor control more arenas of their lives, they can move out of poverty.

In this effort the role of the state which has a contractual obligation to ensure an equitable world for ever one of its citizens, not the least for the impoverished, is very crucial. In fact the tremendous faith vested in the state by the poor storied here in this study is only matched by the state's contemptuous rebuff of this 'natural' congruence of interests. While the state is cosying up to the market, the market is sworn to make the state wither away. It is only the poor who have a stake in strengthening the state—provided the state fulfils the role that it was meant to do: secure, enhance and protect the rights of the most vulnerable. The withdrawal of the state from its welfare functions in this era of globalisation is now a reality and has been commented upon. What these stories show is also the inability of the state to fulfil those functions even when it wants to.

The case of poverty alleviation efforts by one of the non-state actors, namely, the NGOs, too is not very encouraging. Their micro-credit programmes have run aground when aimed at carrying the poor from the ocean of poverty to the shore of well-being. Despite the hype of the micro-credit proponents, micro-credit does not reach the absolute poor. When it does, it soon becomes apparent that they do not have the capacity to repay the loans. A distressing finding is that the poor take loans fully knowing they are getting into the debt trap. They do so to get back to the state of absolute poverty! They borrow in the present, and repay in the future with their produce/labour or with themselves and their children. The money is used for handing crises most often, usually in restoring previous survival positions. Being so much on the edges of survival, they are often pushed even lower than absolute poverty by even a small sickness of themselves or their dependents. Their labouring bodies being their only capital, even a day out of work means loss of their 'absolute poor' status into an even more acute state. Their loans are therefore to get back to where they were before—to restore status quo ante as it were. This also shows why the micro-credit programme, with its emphasis on repayment etc—will not work for the absolute poor.

These apart the emerging realities at other levels (regional, national, global) and layers (individual, familial, societal), and the processes they have unleashed are contributing to the increasing irresponsibility of all the structures and institutions otherwise ought to be responsible. This leads to increasing invisibilisation, criminalisation and custodialisation of the poor and the emergence of a clearly pro-nonpoor social order that tends to organise the mainstream society clearly in favour non-poor and obviously against the impoverished population. It is indeed by clearing the society of the latter, the society for the former is sought to be created. The war against poverty has transmogrified into a war against the poor, the irritating and dirty presence in the eyes of those who want a porcelain clean, sanitised world. The poor in most of the life stories are victims of this war manifested in the form of death of compassion, criminalising laws and legislations and anti-poor town planning etc. There is an urgent need to reorganise the war against poor in line with its original mission, viz., war against poverty and more correctly against impoverishing processes.

The skewed war against poor floats the following myths about poor as incontestable truths. These myths build the hatred for the poor in the minds of the nonpoor. Our reconfigured development research therefore should shatter the following myths:

- **The poor are poor because they are lazy**: This is a myth that has been proven wrong many times before too. The book shows that the poor actually work more than the rich, not less. Moreover—in an interesting insight—it also shows that the poor are willing to work more. Throughout the engagement with the life stories, one cannot miss out on the agility and dynamism of the impoverished individuals. They are constantly on the move in search water, work, food and health facilities. They are engaged in one other activity, all not necessarily aimed at earning money. Even the old do not shun work.

- **The poor have no shame**: The yearning for dignity, even more than life itself, is forcefully brought out. The poor get into debt, they work as slaves, because they do not want to have to beg or do demeaning work. The women becoming sex workers is the outcome of limited range of choice available to her to earn her money with dignity as well as the consequence of anti-women value system prevailing in the society which sees her only as pleasure-yielding flesh. Similarly in many others cases of sub-human and 'immoral' choices made by the poor, it is the lack of other choices that force them to resort to what they eventually do. It is only when other dignity-enhancing coping mechanisms are denied to them that they beg and let the work enter into them or let those whom they are bound to protect and nurture also get back into the 'job market.' In these life–stories, moments of happiness and hope centre around the time when the people are acknowledged as human beings, with the capacity to creatively use their mind and their body as a whole in seeking livelihood or exercising their agency.

- **The poor are habitual liars**. The 'lies' that the poor tell are survival mechanisms. These 'lies' are not only in their dealings with others—which are often to ensure that they get the minimum resources to survive through acts of grace—but also to themselves to retain their dignity; their many denial mechanisms to ensure that they retain their dignity at least in their own lives. Wilfully talking of their body intrusive jobs as 'temporary,' elaborate cleaning of the house, its courtyard and rooms even when these are all imaginary in a one-room pavement house, all are part of the quest for dignity.

- **The poor are dumb and uncreative**: The poor have different markers to their time and space. To make meaning of their life, they make differences. For instance a beggar divides his time among various railway stations for each of the activities he does; the homeless people in Chennai (Madras) city in India, we find the conversion of the street edges into homes with clearly demarcated spaces for bedrooms, thresholds etc; a sex worker inverts the 'inferior' and exploitative social role and structures by calling her work 'fieldwork' or 'going on line' or 'entertainment business' or 'going for dance'. The scavenger woman calls her work 'municipality work'. The street boy forced out of his home to earn a living for his family calls it a 'choice'. Beggars call their work 'Money catching' or 'earning'. They use these categories of defining their work as a response against the stigma and degradation that they are subjected to. Shelterless people establish neatly circumscribed homes on pavements and other open public spaces. These homes that are for most part imaginary, have carefully worked out kitchens, sleeping rooms and doorsteps. They are maintained with religious rigour—sprinkling water in the 'front yard'; keeping the place clean and tidy. These imaginary homes are completely real within the minds of the shelterless, even if their worth and security in real terms are minimal.

Fighting against these myths is only a part of the process of moving towards the horizon of manifold possibilities. Rights-based and solidarity-demonstrating approaches are an integral part of the solution. Larger actors like state have to work towards harnessing the positive energies and processes at all levels. Information and technology revolution offers both possibilities and challenges. While the poor are consistently stood by in their efforts to reap benefits out of all modern and post-modern processes by the responsibility-wielding structures, the latter should also show solidarity with and shield the poor when they are negatively impacted by the same processes. This requires a rethinking on the strategies for the warfare against poverty and impoverishment.

All along even the many of the radical groups waged the war against poverty without involving the poor themselves consistently and fully. Even when involving them, they were led by the non-poor who visualised what is a better world for the poor. Thus the poor were mere tools in the hands of the non-poor. Though spectacular results were achieved as result of these non-poor led wars, they could not sustain themselves and ensure justice across time, space and different categories of people. In the third instance, the war was organised with the conviction that the poor cannot be allies as they themselves do not detest poverty. It was assumed that it is incumbent upon the non-poor, who hate poverty and wish to eliminate it from this world, who have to battle it out on their own against poverty. The history hitherto has been dominated by one or other of the above three types of war against poverty. The consequences are devastating as confirmed by the stories. Any autonomous and indigenous efforts and strategies evolved by the poor to cope with their poverty were contemptuously treated and never shown solidarity with by the warmongers. One of the important casualties was the myriad of organisations or groupings that they built from time to time. Their native associational life has been absolutely delegitimised and accorded not even an iota of political significance, if they do not conform to the rigour of modern political institutional standards and practices. There is an immediate urgency for creating space for enhanced associational life among the poor and standing by and according transformative identity to the groupings, and organisations and movements arising thereof. It is in these spheres we all come to realise as to how much hatred the poor themselves have for poverty and the burning desire to get out of it. There begins the collective efforts at redemption.

At the organisational level, too different responses must be evolved. If poverty is the symptom of structures of social relations, ranging from the micro level dyadic relationship between individuals to macro level relationship between institutions /organisations with individuals/ groups, then the changes have to begin at both levels. One step would be to embed the culture of listening into the organisation. It is certainly not to mass produce qualitative research projects. Acknowledging the equal humanity of even the poorest and respecting their personhood should be the organisational foundation. Programming to reflect their priorities, and enhance their dignity at all times thus becomes the core organisational mission. The challenge lies in turning these core values into organisational relationships and action.

At the collective levels, development organisations should involve the voices of the unheard population as a mandatory determinant of its strategies and programmes. Consultation with the impoverished becomes the essential component of planning and strategising. The expert opinion is significant only to the extent that it is confirmed or invalidated by the distilled opinion of the impoverished. This necessitates the acquisition of a plethora of perspectives and variety of expertise on the part of the organisation and its staff, mostly derivative of intense engagement with people's lives rather than just from other disengaged epistemic sources. Concomitant to this would be the radical revision of our existing development wisdom by rubbing them against the perspectives and lived experiences of the impoverished and marginalised. This would require creating or drawing upon a database of people's voices as they speak of their experiences. This entails a learning-action loop: start from people and end with them. An enhanced and intense engagement with people's lives without an air of dominance and patronage is what should be the resulting practice of this exercise.

At the larger societal level, the organisation has to involve in responsibility-restoring measures by joining hands with newly-vitalised peoples organisations (sometimes even allowing them to lead the processes), civil society groups at both national and international levels as well as by fostering people to people solidarity and connections. Apart from internationalisation of organisational energies, internationalisation of solidarity of the local people is required.

Organisations working for development, will have to learn from the wisdom of the people's lives that NGOs cannot dream of substituting responsibility-wielding structures/organisations/institutions such as nation-states or even families. In a world where manifold possibilities of equitable living and being is fast drying up or portrayed only as a mirage by the vested interests, development organisations have to have the conviction about the multiple possibilities, by demonstrating their efficacy, affordability, normalcy and practicality. This requires sustained engagement with people who are impoverished, marginalised and criminalised as their lived lives are the wellsprings of such alternate possibilities.

Conclusion

Poverty research is inevitably tied to the aspirations of policy-making as they are concerned about propelling actions. But the last few decades of policy making and the actions resulting out of it, duly assisted by action research of the development studies, have compelled many of the sensitive ones among us to conclude that a lot of bad actions is much worse than no action at all. It was because the action research and the consequent actions were guided by much of self-serving notion and assumptions elaborated above in this essay.

End Notes:

[1] Ashis Nandy: The Beautiful, Expanding Future of Poverty: Popular Economics as a Psychological Defense: *International Studies Review, Vol. 4, No. 2, International Relations and the New Inequality (Summer, 2002)*, p. 115

[2] Ibid. p. 115

[3] Maia Green: Representing Poverty And Attacking Representations: Some Anthropological Perspectives On Poverty In Development: GPRG-WPS-009, accessed at http://www.gprg.org/. p.12

[4] It has been stated differently by Goode and Maskovsky who treat "Poverty as a political, economical, and ideological effect of capitalist processes and state activity. poverty as a function of power, as an essential and utterly predictable effect of the ideological and political-economic processes of late capitalism". The New Poverty Studies: The Ethnography of Power, Politics, and Impoverished People in the United States, edited by Judith Goode and Jeff Maskovsky. New York: New York University Press, 2001. p.3

[5] The poverty sector is viewed as a distinct entity with stable internal characteristics whose study will reveal the causes of poverty (Yapa 1996a). The point of such a study is to devise operational methods that will help 'solve' the problem. This is what I mean by reification of poverty: the lack of basic needs by large numbers of people has been transformed into a quantifiable poverty problem existing in a distinct and coherent sector with

stable inner characteristics, the study of which will reveal the causes of poverty and thus help us to find solutions. *Lakshman Yapa*: The Poverty Discourse and the Poor in Sri Lanka: *Transactions of the Institute of British Geographers, New Series, Vol. 23, No. 1 (1998),pp. 95-115*

[6]*Ibid, p 99*

[7] G. K. Lieten Faltering Development and the Post-Modernist Discourse: *Social Scientist*, Vol. 30, No. 7

[8]*Booth, D, Leach, M & Tierney, A 1999 Experiencing Poverty in Africa: Perspectives from Anthropology, Background paper No 1 b for the World Bank Poverty Status report 1999.*

[9] Dube. S C (1994): *'Understanding Poverty', Tradition and Development*, New Delhi.

[10]*P. C. Joshi, Perspectives on Poverty and Social Change: The Emergence of the Poor as a Class: Economic and Political Weekly, Vol. 14, No. 7/8, Annual Number: Class and Caste in India (Feb., 1979), pp. 355-357+359+361+363+365-366*

[11] Like Durkeim's lamentation about Anomie, Marx's notion of Alienation and Weber's Iron Cage.

[12] See Satish Saberwal, Sociologists and Inequality in India: The Historical Context: *Economic and Political Weekly,* Vol. 14, No. 7/8, Annual Number: Class and Caste in India (Feb., 1979), pp. 243-245+247+249+251+253-254

[13] See, M. N. Srinivas, Development of Sociology in India: An Overview, *Economic and Political Weekly,* Vol. 22, No. 4 (Jan. 24, 1987), pp. 135-138

[14] Jaganath Pathy: Imperialism, Anthropology and the Third World: *Economic and Political Weekly,* Vol. 16, No. 14 (Apr. 4, 1981), pp. 623-627

[15] N. Krishnan Namboodiri :On Sociology in India: Yesterday, Today, and Tomorrow Author(s): Source: Social Forces, Vol. 59, No. 1 (Sep., 1980), p. 288

III

Listening As a Radical Act: The Art of Life Story Collection

Introduction

Listening is an act of humility. It can be humbling too. However listening in the everyday life circumstances of the poor is a weak act, a practice condemned to be followed by the poor, marginalized and the oppressed. Normally it is women in relation to men, Dalits in relation to the non-Dalits and children in relation to adults who are forced to cultivate listening as a skill. In a scaled up version, even the larger research agendas fashioned as science, only reiterated listening as a weak act or act of the weak by compelling the respondents in the research exercises to fit into the designs evolved in circumstances alien to the 'respondents'.

Our commitment to situate the act of listening at the heart of participatory research exercises arises from the compelling necessity to transform the otherwise weak act of listening into a radical act. It is precisely because of this commitment that we hold listening as a cardinal value through in any social research endeavours. By taking up the weak act of listening, we want to humble ourselves as well as to translate that into a radical act. Let us consider the following:

1. Listening is a radical act in the development research primarily for it calls for repositioning of social actors. It presupposes altering and restructuring social relations and interaction patterns, first in the domain of research and later, by extension, in the domain of wider society.

2. Listening is a radical act in research exercise, for it is done not so much for confirmations of the researchers' opinion, but for refutation. This has to be read in the background of how participatory approaches have been used by many development agencies and researchers to confirm their frameworks rather than radically challenge them. The boring uniformity of conclusions arrived at by PPA studies about the perceptions of poverty across the globe, despite the expansive multidimensionality, only buttresses our argument that, if they had been conducted with listening as a value, then they would have led to the breakdown of many paradigms on poverty, rather than presenting them as manageable data. If our studies on poor done in the form of life story collections have merely confirmed that "here is one more poor who is starving", that would be tantamount to an ornithologist declaring that she has found "another crow that is black". Philosopher of knowledge Karl Popper would argue as to how our modern-day scientists are suffering from a particular form of a neurosis, due to which they get nervous when anything or any event that breaks down the regular occurrences of the natural phenomena they are researching. They declare them as background noises and discount them from readings in experiments. They are "insignificant happenings" that cannot have any relevance for the research. Since then they are never "listened to" by the rest of the members of the scientific community, who are engaged in repeating the experiments only to confirm the existing paradigms. This is because, Popper concludes, they are engaged in *confirmation* research rather than *refutation* research (Popper, 1969). Only when the paradigm is held in doubt will we be engaged in refutations research. And only when we look for falsifying cases that would challenge our time-honoured paradigms, will we start listening to even the minutest of the noises. There commences a creative humane falsifying research. It is humane because the moment the existing paradigms are kept in doubt, the certainty and arrogance arising out of holding on to them steadfastly, disappear. And as persuasively argued by Zygmunt Bauman, violence abates. Bauman

says that many destructive mass murders such as Holocaust have happened because the perpetrators believed in the axiomatic character of the paradigms they had believed and obeyed. They did not hold their paradigms in suspicion not even for a second. Listening was dead there (Bauman, 2001). By the same token we can argue that much of the development violence indeed has been the outcome of such certainty cherished by the development agencies. Even when the flexibility of such wisdom is admitted by the development professionals, at the end of every round of PRA, or other qualitative research initiatives, the wisdom gets only solidified further, except for some elemental changes on facts and points of view. The paradigm shift itself has not occurred in the very conceptualization of poverty. What has occurred instead is the expansion of the definition to include very many qualitative aspects to it. Listening was dead there too.

3. Listening is a radical act in another count too. When 'listening to', we witness the evolution of stories narrated with the desire for coherence, arguably, for the first time in the lives of many poor. Yet it is not a charitable admission of the story to take shape. It is a very natural outcome of listening, even when there is no conscious intention meant for it. This is very crucial because the act of listening subsumes or ought to be subsumed by different conception of humans as storying persons. Indeed it is a different ontological reality we posit to human being in line with many narrative analysts. It is to these aspects we turn our attention now.

I Tell Stories, Therefore I Am

Human beings live storiable lives. It is in the act of storying that they find their essence**. By rephrasing the classical Marxian phrase we can say "Humans are essentially storying animals." In our research too we believe that, more often than not, the evolution of these stories is a joint exercise between the researcher and the person listened to. The fact that a storiable life can be grasped by the poor has a radical potential to transform people into humans. But the initial reluctance or even inability to coherently narrate their stories of life in many of the poor person we met only suggested that there was a breakdown in their self conceptions as humans. The arguments of Veena Das (1990), in her excellent essay on Bhopal Gas victims, that the absence of narration in the lives of the humans signifies the breakdown or disorganization of their personal selves are very relevant here. When trauma strikes, narratability is the casualty. And the return of the story to the persons is the moment of triumph of the person over the objective history, because by recuperating a story of ourselves, we personalize the historical time and space as ours own. Listening can create those triumphant moments for others whose stories were never organized before. Yet listening should not be construed as a charitable act by which the restoration of humanness in the poor through their recovery of storiability is a *gift* from the researcher to the poor. In contrast, listening has to herald an authentic meeting between authentic people as R.D.Laing (1990) would propose.

The astounding fact that listening ends up constituting the humanness in the other, is very important for it can radicalize PRA methods themselves. The extraordinary or proclaimed sensitivity to people's way of world-making notwithstanding, PRA methods have not seen the poor as *storying persons* inasmuch they saw them as *speaking persons*. The total reliance on the poor people's self-chosen modes and ways of revealing information could not still help PRA methodologies to overcome their obsession with information in whatever forms they came – be it stories, diagrams, or answers to interviews. This has not enabled the poor to construct an ordered narration of themselves, as they only saw themselves as information-provides under howmuchever democratic or enabling environment it happened. The unintended breakdown of stories that was recurringly produced by however sincere application of PRA methods, failed to restore the essential human quality, namely as storying persons. It could also be attributed to the failure of the PRA to transfer the foundational values guiding them to the people it studied.

Thus, by foregrounding listening as a value, we aspire to turn the research exercise into a joint human enterprise. In this, humans emerge as storying individuals. Stories themselves can be an extraordinarily significant source of details in retrospect, because stories of the poor are invariably enmeshed in history. We shall elaborate on this a bit more now.

Stories as Histories

C.W. Mills (1959, p.2) in his book Sociological Imagination, talks very evocatively about the birth of sociological imagination at the intersection between an individual's biography and the history of the society that individual belongs to[5]. Juxtapose this to ethnographers' understanding of folk narratives wherein the confluence of the history in its luminous presentness, occurs with the past of the mythic recited, even when that recital looks highly personal. What we get is a renewed understanding of stories as rich documents about the persons narrating them as well as the society that person belongs to. In a research done among the traditional singer women in Tamil Nadu who sing the lamentation songs Margaret Trawick (1991) found that in singing wailing songs, the poor woman continuous to infuse her personal grief into an otherwise publicly acceptable content of the songs. Trawick called it narrative isomorphism to suggest how personal can be public and public can be personalized. They are situations in which the personal narrative tends always to carry the traces of the history of the society and this has been well documented in anthropology.

Characterizing life stories not merely as personal narratives, but as narratives of wider social context, Kothari (Kothari and Hulme, 2003, p. 4) writes, "Crucially individual stories draw upon collective imaginations and themes as they must, since life stories are inevitably located in the social context of meanings, languages and institutional and national cultures. In this way the storied self becomes inserted into collective narratives." Not only that, there are extremely critical energies to be found in the stories as Kothari (ibid, p.4) argues, "The life stories can also illuminate those aspects of people's lives that are not normally revealed and in so doing, provide a valuable critique of development policy ..."

This understanding helps us to derive immense amount of inspiration to see the stories of the people not simply as personal accounts of themselves, but as carriers of history of the society at large. Essentially listening is an important component of sociological imagination, for it impels the researcher to see multiple meeting points between individuals' biography and public history (Mills 1959, p.2). Not merely that, but a radical act of listening also helps us to appreciate the meaning-making strategies of the people who creatively personalize what is a public experience. By doing this we consummate the authentic relationship by centering human agency of the poor, apart from facilitating the constitution of mutual humanity of both actors – the researcher and the narrator. It is in this context, we prioritise listening, not so much *to* dehumanizing piecemeal information, but *to* humanizing stories.

These apart, the choice for life stories as the source of data has been guided by the inherent merit of the life stories. We refrain from elaborating on them as much of the merits of collecting life stories and the series of positive or critical effects it could have on the development debate and wisdom have already been elaborated extensively both in the related literature (Slim and Thomson, 1993) and in the LPP training manual of Actionaid India (*LPP Training Manual –I*, actionaid India, 2001, Mimeo).

Listening in Participatory Approaches

The very purpose of bringing the act of listening to the centre stage of the research exercise in the social research is tempered by two critical discomfitures we have with the current modes of researching in development sector.

1. Firstly, research in development sector has been conceived of as an independent activity set apart from on-the-field development engagement one has with the people. At best, development research can only qualify and inform such engagement, even while maintaining its aloofness from development practice. This, in essence, boiled down to mean that research itself is not a development practice in its own right. Furthermore, whereas the conclusions of the research may call for transformation, modification and alteration in development practice and *seldom* in the behavioural aspects of the development practitioners, the research enterprise itself does not warrant such radical transformation in behaviours, attitudes and dispositions on the part of the researchers. This was because for long research in development sector was done by experts in quantitative techniques who hailed from outside development sector. While the experts' findings called for changes in the development practice, the experts themselves went out of the research exercise unchanged. What is even worse, for these expert researchers another engagement in research only confirms their certainty about the infallibility of their knowledge and techniques. Both the researcher and the research do not listen to or learn from what such intense engagements with people might tell.[2] Against this, therefore, we envisage a research exercise that in itself *is* a development practice calling for the involvement of development practioners and development actors rather than experts on the one hand and subsequent transformation in their own development practice and engagement with

the people with whom they work, on the other hand.

2. Our second discomfiture is with the way even some of the alternatives have failed to live up to the promise they showed initially. The arrival of action research gave tremendous optimism as it aspired to establish research as development action in its own right. It brought into currency refreshing new tools and methodologies which promised to make research itself a transformative development action leaving both the researchers and the researched significantly changed in its wake – behaviourally and attitudinally. Central to such research endeavour are the participatory approaches and tools. However much of the criticisms leveled against many participatory methods point to the fact that while listening to the voices of the poor by deploying focused group discussions or interviews or even other PRA tools, the act of listening was given as much significance as perhaps notes-taking, prompting and other such gamut of acts that formed part of application of PRA methods. Listening as a cardinally humbling act has always got drowned in the midst of these other 'technical acts' – whether instinctual or cultivated. In fact, the root cause of a host of problems associated with participatory methods concerning their having been used predominantly for assessing the needs of the poor; legitimating the end of the agencies and actors who primarily applied it and; their lending themselves easily to be mastered and monopolized by big donor agencies and so on and so forth, can be traced to the absence of the art of listening as a governing value, or to its reduction to a marginal instinctual act in the process of relating to the poor.

During the last three decades so much of participatory exercises have been conducted in the development sector to persuade a critic to pithily remark that there will be only few rare groups of people who would not have been PRAed (Green, 2003). It can be even pointed out that in the same period almost all the development organisation have taken to participatory approaches, so much so that they have become a mandatory part of project life cycles and even institutional style. But a highly self-reflexive exercise on the part of these organisations to asses the extent of internalizations of the cardinal values such as 'participation', 'equality', 'mutual learning' etc that govern participatory approaches has rarely been undertaken. By the same token, the marginal presence of these cardinal values in the everyday life circumstances of the poor who have been repeatedly subjected to PRA initiatives, not only point to the inequal structural relationship between the local people and the PRA experts but can itself be an indication of the failure of the development practice.

We wish to argue that despite reasonable claims of participatory methods to remain proximate to the lifeworld of the poor in making choices about tools, such as diagrams, use of native objects, narrations etc., the sustained application of them in the development practice has only reduced them to *techniques*, instead of translating into *values*. We believe that it is because the prevalent modes of undertaking participatory methods and tools have not paid close attention to an anthropological understanding of the values and logic that govern the speech-acts and interaction patterns among the local people (Green, 2002). The swift and uniform application of many of the participatory tools among a diverse range of communities across the globe without ensuring their relevance and acceptance for the members of the communities has only meant that many of the crucial native social acts and logic have been lost sight of. Listening is one such value and act finding recurring salience among the poor but has been grossly converted into a marginal act in the practice of participatory methods. One indication of how 'listening' is understood more in an instrumental sense than as a value is the choice of the phrase used in relation to consultation with poor exercise undertaken by World Bank. In the background paper to World Bank's initiative on Voices of the Poor initiative, Norton and Francis calls for the evolution of "listening devices' to local level experiences, perceptions and analysis to speak to the national level debate and social policy" (Norton and Francis (1992), p.9).

Participatory Methods: The Promises Unfulfilled

The trends mentioned above suggested that 'listening' may become a radical act. Yet even while the three decades of experiences with participatory research attest to many instances of poor people *speaking*, the marginalized *voicing* and the oppressed *inscribing their presence* in the research practices, the evidences to clinch the arguments in favour of *'listening'* are sadly far fewer, if not rare. It can be concluded that all these assertions and speaking on the part of the poor have happened in environments in which *listening* was so much absent as only *hearing* was present. Hearing is essentially a charitable act and not an equalizing or empowering act like listening. Hearing is always a selective act too. As argued by many critics of PRA, the researchers and the agencies that used participatory initiatives have done so as to hear what they have always wanted to 'hear' and confirm for legitimating their own agendas. Echoing this Ruggeri Laderchi (2001, pp. 5, 6) writes as to how participation and participatory methods have become compatible to support the market oriented economic paradigm when it should have challenged it in reality. She mentions " the developments in participatory research have been described as ways in which the participatory research agenda has been co-opted for instrumental ends by new converts [such as World Bank], while the extent to which the consultations have been participatory has been questioned."

The application of various PRA techniques across the globe though has thrown light on the differential and multidimensional experiences of the poor, the striking similarity and uniformity of such pluralistic experiences of the poor in different regions and nations call into question the fundamental assumption and notions that guide data collection. Is it because the processes of dissemination of PRA techniques onto various development professionals and practioners encourage only singular mode of conceptualizing poverty as deemed fit and relevant by powerful institutions and forces that are not even geographically located in poor countries? Or is it just that the development practitioners ask the same questions everywhere despite deploying myriad of techniques and tools? The answer is certainly not the global solidarity of all the poor in the world, nor surely the singularity of their experiences however multi-layered may they be.

If poverty experiences of the poor have acquired somewhat seamless uniformity and consensual standardization, it does not mean that, in reality, the poor people's lives are such, but it means the triumph of the manageability-of-poverty anxiety on the part of the agencies who applied these methods. This is corroborated by a recent analysis of the PPA documents conducted in Africa as a prelude to the largest ever PPA exercise undertaken by any one person or agency namely, the World Bank's Voices of Poor study. While the study enriched our understanding of the poor and poverty, what was ultimately presented themselves were highly selective information that suited the larger interest of the sponsoring organisation. "The preliminary PPA document had noted certain themes that have not been highlighted in the main overviews of PPA results. However what is perhaps more striking is what is missing even from the expanded list. There are a range of other issues for poverty analysis that seem important *a priori* but are notably absent in the first round PPAs. The selectivity at various levels due for example to pressures on writers of country synthesis reports to highlight findings that have immediacy for policy makers or the indirect influence of the strategies policy framework adopted by the World Bank on the way themes are organized" (ibid, p.9)

Indeed much of the development knowledge doubled the strength of their arrogance using participatory research methods, because of their inherent amenability to such instrumentally and politically-motivated selectivity – people in margin could only confirm the belief systems of the development agents, their refutations are regarded as background noises. This, we propose, is the result of 'hearing'. What is needed is a movement towards 'listening'.

Poverty and Beyond

If we aspire to radicalize the otherwise weak act of listening in this research exercise, it cannot happen in the absence of radicalized conception of poverty. We may have to make very clear as to what is the operational notion of poverty we use in this research. It would be fair to say that there was a certain degree of predetermination of specific conditions of poverty under which the people we collected stories from lived. These conditions were both hypothetical as well as 'educated guesses' based on our previous experiences of working with people – many of which were highly personal encounters with individual people living in such conditions.

Operationally we are taking poverty to mean 'impoverishment'[2] in that poverty is an outcome of a range of impoverishing processes. Unlike the term poverty, which imputes the culpability for being poor to the impoverished people, impoverishment locates the problem in the structure of social, economic and political relations into which the impoverished are forced on inequal terms. This accounts for our agreed parameters for the listening contexts centering around conditions, rather than on the traits and attributes of being poor. We were cautious not to end up describing the poor, but only the conditions that surround them. Doing the former would have only strengthened already solidified notions of who the poor are.

We are very uncomfortable with the tendency in many poverty studies to describe poverty by describing the poor. Those studies end up constructing a personality of poor while attempting to understand the phenomenon of poverty. This manner of locating poverty in the personality of the poor tends to posit poverty as the personal problem and failure of the poor. This also imputes an element of passivity to the poor as the essential agents of their own poverty. We firmly believe poverty is much more than starvation and whole panoply of attributes given to it.

Poverty studies also have another tendency, which we wish to distance ourselves from, i.e., solidification of poverty as a 'thing' in itself as if it is an objectified reality outside that can be singled out and attacked[3]. As much of the development practice and wisdom is aiming at constituting a 'thing' called poverty, it tends to hold every experience of the poor as contributing to such constitution. Even the most challenging and against-the-grain experience of the poor, though may shake the complacency of the existing ideas on poverty, does not fundamentally uproot the edifice on which such existing wisdoms were erected. This objectification of poverty results in treating poverty as the disease to be instantly eliminated whereas it is only a symptom of the prevailing socio-economic political relations in the society.

The clarion call given by many critiques of development ideology that one ought to move beyond a thing called 'poverty' and problematise the wealth-making practices of rich will go unlistened to as long as 'hearing' for confirmation dominates development research. It is our belief that listening to the poor is one such exercise, wherein we held forth our conception of poverty for falsification. We do not know how far we have moved forward in the terrain beyond objectified poverty, but we are willing to allow that challenge to be posed to the prevailing conception.

Why the Most Marginalised and the Poorest?

With this revised understanding of poverty as impoverishment we need to commit ourselves to collecting stories of individuals who are the most marginalised and poorest. In choosing to listen to poor and the most marginalized among we aspired to effect two crucial corrections. One is our discomfiture with participatory poverty assessments or PRAs, that have excluded from their ambit those categories of the populations characterised as the poorest even by the poor themselves. Despite the best intentions of these methods to privilege the local voices, they have often excluded the most marginalized among them, namely widows, disabled, mentally ill, beggars, homeless. Here it is instructive to appreciate the conclusions arrived at by Mick Moore and others who have reviewed the whole range of participatory studies done hitherto. They conclude, "It is reasonable to infer that there is often a wide diversity of views and understandings about the causes of poverty among the poorest people themselves. We are not very well informed about that, partly because it is the very poorest whose voices are the least likely to be heard in any investigation. A great deal of experience indicates that the very poorest people tend to be under-represented as respondents in any kind of research unless very conscious efforts are made include them.... It is very likely that the voices of the very poor that we do hear are rarely those of the sick, old, disabled, shy, shunned or inarticulate." Even in those cases wherein they have been included, the specificities of individual experiences that could have high critical potency have been lost due to the inherent bias of the participatory methods to work with groups and present a seamless, consensual perceptions of the groups, albeit the plurality of such perceptions. Life story approach and the intense listening it presupposes, take as closer to the individual experiences of his/her situations and brings refreshingly critical input even into the conclusions arrived at by PPAs or PRAs.

Even when focusing on the excluded groups we were more concerned about the conditions that prevail around the impoverished people – conditions that push them into poverty, sustain them and conditions that would get them out eventually, than describing the persons themselves. These were sought to be realised under non-negotiable cardinal values -- listening, relating to the impoverished because it is fair in its own right, being the most crucial among them. Instead of arriving at standardisable, measurable and conclusive understanding on poverty or even poor persons (in the development literature one would find inexhaustible descriptions of poor and poverty), we aspired to listen to the multiplicity of the impoverishing process as narrated by the poor.

Our commitment to listening to people so as to collect their stories is also influenced by some of the strident criticisms of existing modes of conceptualizing poverty. It can be argued that the resurrection of multidimensionality and plurality of experiences of poverty experiences from the invisibility to which they have been condemned till now, are the outcome of *not* those quantitative surveys or *even* the PPA exercises *but* of some sensitive minds meeting with the invisibilised poor in purely personal encounters. It is these chance occurrences that have triggered more extensive and deeper exploration of the conditions of invisible people in a much more systematic and formal manner. Listening to poor persons' stories is born out of such optimism to restage and reenact such chance occurrences in a systematic and formalized manner. That explains why in our collections of stories they are more number of people who would have been missed by even the most sensitive PPA initiatives so far – there are many beggars, sex workers, disabled, mentally ill, prisoners, leprosy patients, street children, HIV/ AIDS patients religious mendicants, eunuchs and many others not visible to the noblest poverty researcher. In these personal encounters with invisibilised people we can learn about the extraordinary intensity of lives lived, creativity exercised in restoring dignity to themselves. There can also be stringent criticism about the existing institutional arrangement and policies too.

The Co-Authored Stories

Consequently the stories thus collected will turn out to be predominately about two important aspects. Firstly it is about how their being in conditions of poverty is not their making or personal failure, but traceable to conditions and processes external to them over which they have least or no control. Secondly it is about how they are coping with/in these impoverishing situations creatively, dignifiedly and courageously, though most such life strategies have often been criminalized, contemptuously treated and unrewarded by the wider society.

It was very stunning to find out the refreshingly equalizing potency of entering into listening exercises and collaborative authoring on poverty in the process of conducting life story collection. Much against many other extractive research exercises that vested primary authorship (including the analysis) in the researcher, we sought to retain the authorship predominately with the impoverished people. It was startling to discover what the impoverished persons chose to discuss, highlight, and what they glossed over. We do not intend to say more about the exact content of the stories, as it would amount to entering into an analytical exercise, though there is a lot of temptation to do so.

If we are content with abstaining from rolling the narratives of the impoverished masses into manageable information for the planners and policy makers, it is guided by two imperatives. One, as stated elsewhere, we have to present the intensity of the life of the poor in its diversity and plurality without standardizing them to mediated data; the second, any such perspective-building for planning and strategizing cannot happen in the absence of the poor persons who shared their stories with us – the impoverished are not just *purveyors* of raw material for perspective-building, but can be allies in such process itself.

Hence, in what follows we will discuss the steps involved in collection and analysis of life stories as they stand in the forms in which they will be collected by the researchers. Life stories, though they are mediated by the experiences/ perspectives of the researchers, they more or less remain as co-authored stories with the researcher limiting her authorship to the minimal. This is the first step. As a second step an analytical report and the learning from the stories will have to be visualized as a joint exercise between the poor and activist researchers in much the same way story collection processes happens. Even if the written stories are demonstrative of the fact such analysis has happened indeed, in the form of one-to-one interaction between the researcher and the coresearcher, for all other 'conditions' that characterize the life of the poor, there will be self-evident scenarios and details in the stories themselves. Hence it needs to be left to the imaginations of the readers to glean inferences and insights about the meanings of life in poverty for the poor. Allowing the stories to speak for themselves absolves us also from the crime of extractive stance adopted by many participatory exercises, particularly when they have implication for policy formulation and organisational evaluation.

If at the end of reading the stories one arrives at a different understanding of poor persons, their agency, their creativity, their coping abilities, they must be taken as an outcome of a triumph of the collaborative authorship that emerged between the speaking and the listening persons. Surely they are not the results of condescending or concessional gesture from us. Indeed we need not aim at recasting the image of poor in a positive light, as it would be as patronizing in much the same way as the opposite constructs are demeaning.

The Lessons Learnt

The very evocative nature of life story collection governed by listening as an equalizing value intrinsically resists any prescriptive procedures being imposed upon them. It is in that light the following points have to be understood. The various processes adopted in the collection of stories have to be highly contextual and intuitive, so there cannot be any uniform methods of collecting life stories. The following present the dilemmas and many solutions, again not applicable to all situations universally. The readers can take them as suggestions. A bit of caveat: Some of the points are reiterations.

<u>Why Listen?</u>

Listening to the voices of people in poverty is an effort to understand why hunger and poverty still exists. It is based on the belief that the people who can lead the human race out of poverty and move forward are the people who have experienced it.

The idea of "listening to the poor people" is by no means new to the development sector. Participation has been at the heart of most of what has been considered progressive and effective in the field to date. Over time, different people have recognized that participation – the process by which more and more people come together and decide their lives when they choose to – is crucial for social evolution to occur. The idea has two concepts – the concept of listening and human relatedness and the concept of poverty. Poverty, because it pervades human existence and causes untold misery to most of the people on this planet and listening, because it is an important method of beginning to untangle our ways out of the situation, we are in.

Objectives

The first derivative outcome of listening to people in poverty gaining a deeply reflective understanding of issues of poverty, marginalisation, exclusion, deprivation and injustice, with people who are poor through conversations about their experiences and perceptions. By listening to their voices and reflecting on their experiences, we may gain invaluable and fresh insights about poverty seen through the lenses of their own perceptions. These would include insights into coping mechanisms, the role of external players and forces in their lives as well as the social actors with whom they interface, their aspirations and how they feel these aspirations can be actualised.

The second derivative outcome the institutional and personal reflection on methods and structural of relationship, gained by development organisations and practioners working with people who are poor. Thus, such listening helps us to move away from instrumental target-based programmatic interventions on the part of the institution to interventions based on reflective participative processes with people who live in poverty.

Methodology

The methodology used was that of life stories[1] collected through the formation of 'dyads'. The dyads were to allow the formation of the relation between the members of the institution and the person living in poverty.

Life stories

Life stories as the source of data are chosen for many reasons. The recognition that the human brain is wired to accept and process stories; and that stories abound in human existence – from fairytales and mythology to gossip about the people one interacts with – is one (Denning 2000). There has been increasing focus on stories and narratives on reflection about the human experience in recent times. The opportunity created by using stories more reflectively provides new ways of looking at what has happened and fashion new ways of being that fulfils the human purpose is immense.

Stories are about matters of the heart – emotions that intertwine with thought in producing a complex tapestry of experience. Emotions – how one feels – about an experience are crucial for processes of change and transformation. In a world overwhelmed by bits of information floating around, introducing emotions into the reflective process frees meaning making in creative ways.

Then there are two reasons outlined by Rachel Slater (Slater, 2000). Life stories allow the exploration of peoples' agency over a period of time within the social, economic and political structures they live within. This was crucial in characterising poor people as agents survive and operate on their contexts rather than as 'victims'.

The second is the space provided by this methodology to the people consulted – wherein they define what is important in their lives; the events and experiences that they prioritised in determining what led them into poverty; what keeps them there and what will release them from it. This creation of a common space wherein the person being consulted has the power to determine the events covered serves to reduce the power between the collector of the stories and the person whose story is being recorded.

There are other advantages of individual testimonies as reflective documents. They show the *complexity* of individual experience. The imposition of sectoral divisions between the different aspects of the narrators' lives that other methodologies require need not be imposed. These imposed divisions often erase or contour contradictions and conflict within the data, as well as connections.

These stories pay importance to the reality and repetitiveness of everyday life – the spaces in between significant events which constitute the majority of people's lives. Through bringing in a concept of time and repetition, they allow the individual to reflect on their lives and on poverty as if it were part of a larger unfolding of their lives over time. Thus patterns repeated over and over again in time in daily life that forms part of the narrative of the individual comes to light. This form of reflection contextualised not merely in space but also in time meant that it was possible to see consequences and the direction of future events and the possibility of change.

The nuances of life stories that are dictated by the narrator rather than the collector reveal generally *hidden spheres of experience* (for example, family life), and *hidden connections* (between, say, social relationships and economic decisions, past experience and future priorities). In the development context in particular, it can shed useful light on links and gaps, between policymaking and implementation. (Slim & Thompson 1993: 3; PANOS 1999).

It is this experiential internal reality, as perceived or constructed by the people who have undergone the experiences, that this methodology seeks to capture, rather than an objective 'external' reality.

This very advantage of life story documentation could also be perceived as its primary disadvantage. Even in its best practice, there is no way that the internal reality of one human being can be perceived and documented by another in a clinically detached 'objective' way. It is inevitably a joint quest by two human beings, and whereas the outcome would reflect primarily the experiential reality of one human being, it inevitably would also bear the stamp of the personality, ideology and skills of the other. [refer to the section on 'dyads']

Thus these stories do not have empirical validity as objective truth. However, we believe that subjective reality can never yield 'objective' truths. It has not been our aim to document 'objective' truths since we believe that such truths often overlook, erase or contour human feelings and experiences like humiliation, powerlessness, despair, resignation, anger, aspirations, hope. They also overlook the subjectivities and purposes of people conducting such studies, placing more importance on methodology than purpose.

What we need to do is to write down stories about the lives of the people who live in poverty with whom we converse. In doing so, we understand that we implicate ourselves – what we think, feel, understand and choose to narrate - as much as the person whose story is being narrated. How empathic these are to the experiences and realities of the people that the life story collection seeks to represent then becomes crucial. This lays the responsibility of both rigour and self-reflexivity on the writer.

Thus, the life story analysis is as much about what the narrator feels and has felt, what she experiences and has experienced as about how the writer has been able to perceive, empathise and understand the narrator. Thus in a sense, it is not 'objective' but 'constructed' reality.

Thus the alleged drawbacks of this methodology, that narratives are 'subjective, anecdotal, selective, partial and individual are actually the strengths of the technique because ultimately, they tell us less about the fine details of events and experience than about their *meaning* for people... what people *believe* to be important and true, and why' (Panos 1999; Slim & Thompson 1993: 1).

This then we believe will take us forward in directions we cannot envisage out of our realities.

The Dyad Formation

The dyad of the person from the institution and the person living in poverty is the primary relational context within which the process of reflecting on poverty unfolded. This dyad was an attempt to create a space wherein the inequity created by both power held by traditional and resource based inequities could be negotiated. The recognition that the space was not a "research" space but part of a process of reflection was an attempt to allow the person collecting the life stories to move from a location of a researcher – characterised by objectivity and logic – to a location of a participant while simultaneously freeing the person who was narrating her Life story from the location of the being the "object" of the research.

Three components were essential in the formation of the 'dyad':

First, the **purpose** of the relationship and the space creation between the collector and the poor person had to be clearly outlined, made transparent and consented to by both in the discussion. In determining this, it was essential to differentiate between purpose and agenda. The former allowed the two people to share a common purpose that guides the conversation – in this case to reflect on the life of the poor person and therefore on the phenomenon of poverty. The outcomes of the reflection process were to be of use to both the members. The writer would obtain insights into the phenomenon of poverty while the narrator would be able to reflect on the patterns in her life that would provide creative energy for further negotiation, growth and transformation (Chambers, 1997).

The central relationship was to be built through conversation – a discussion between two people about the topic on hand where each is freely able to express themselves, while allowing it to be guided by the evolving purpose. The life stories then become a record of the conversations and the insights.

Agendas on the other hand are purpose turned into blue-prints – an instrumental determination of the outcome of the relationship. They tend to be lop-sided and force the contours of the relationships into predetermined boundaries wherein the narrator becomes an object rather than a participant.

Thus the collector had to be careful about not slipping into a 'healing' role or a 'research' role, while being conscious that healing and knowledge gathering for and by both participants could well be part of the multiple consequences of the reflection process[2]. However to place either as an agenda would undermine the agency of the narrator since either goal has creates instrumentality in the creation of the conversation and the relation. It would also undermine the possibilities of the collector of the life stories to be healed and to be the source of knowledge to the person living in poverty.

Second, creating these conversational spaces also requires the writer to be sensitive to their own perspectives and values. This **sensitivity** does not mean an erasure of their own values and perspectives – merely a recognition and articulation that they exist, operate within the relations, and are subject to change with evolving experiences and processes. This awareness of one's own values and perspectives allows the writer to table them honestly within the conversational space in as much as the person whose life story is being narrated. Like agenda and purpose, the difference between erasure of subjectivity - perspective and values and recognition of the same is crucial. Attempts at erasure – objectivity - often merely means that the perspectives and values have been hidden and therefore not subject to self-scrutiny as well as reflection within the conversation. It automatically creates hierarchical relations and creates agendas. Recognition and articulation means that the subjectivity of the writer remains in the open arena for discussion, dissent and change. While the former often drains the writer, induces guilt within for the power that he holds and introduces distrust in the relationship, the latter creates a possibility of recognition of dissent and conflict while simultaneously freeing the other to bring in their values and perspectives to the reflection process.

Simultaneously the writer is to be sensitive to process of creating the 'open' space for discussion on the life and experience of poverty. This sensitivity requires him to be conscious of the possible inequities created by his position of power and the way his power determine the reflection process.

The third centred around the recognition of the vulnerability of the narrator. This **vulnerability** is to be differentiated from the vulnerability created by larger exploitative and instrumental structures that people in poverty exist within. It is peculiar to the purpose of the creation of the dyad, wherein the life story of one of its members is the material for reflection, while not requiring the same degree of data sharing from the other member of the dyad. This vulnerability is further accentuated by the fact that the writer is part of a formal institutional framework. Recognition of this vulnerability by both partners of the dyad creates accountability processes in the life story collection and the formation of the dyad; as well as the uses that the data collected is put to.

Finally, if the engagement / relatedness is humanly considerate and clear in purpose between the members of the dyad, such an engagement refreshes and recreates both the people concerned. The purpose of a good conversation within which seeds of thought, curiosity, reflection and action about poverty would be sown. The nurturance of these seeds for both people engaged can then be reflected on further direction. Such a conversation would free both the collector and sharer from determining future direction immediately and would allow each to decide how to proceed further.

Relatedness and Active Listening

The creation of the joint reflective space between the writer and the narrator is essential to create spaces of self-reflexivity about the institution's functioning against the ground perspectives of the issues that poor people contend with. The experience of the poor person as the narrator is considered primary with the role of the analyst being that of a reflector and writer. For this, humility is essential on the part of the story collector.

It is the experience of this writer that wherever real involvement from within the institution and its personnel is present, the stories collected were intense and rewarding. It must be always ensured that the conversational space and life story writing avoids instrumental underpinnings. The balance between instrumentality and reflection and relatedness will remain fragile throughout the story collection exercise with the tilt often towards the former than the latter. Thus, the absorption of core values of humility, relatedness and reflexivity that areto come from the partnership process in story collector is very important.

However, it is not easy to achieve as there are many factors influencing this both at the organisational and personal levels.

The idea of process related work and life stories through creating reflective spaces is new and the exercise itself is in its embryonic stage. Differences between process documentation as reflective tools and research documentation remains unclear in practice, though in theory it is more easily differentiated. Further, the impulse towards programmes and targets within modern contexts is far more powerful than that of reflection and affirmation. The project reflects this tentativeness in its implementation.

Many personnel from many organisations are not normally involved or experienced in the life story writing. There are situations wherein such writing work is often contracted to people specially hired for this purpose. Thus, the

The idea should be one of placing more importance on the process of relatedness rather than the output of stories. The number of stories collected is not that crucial. If number is insisted upon then, the actual writing of the lifestories is liable to become increasingly technical.

To mainstream life story collection, the very process of life story documentation needs to become a central research exercise to be carried out. Thus, the guidelines for the conversation often become guidelines for interviews. With this blurring, the extractive potential of this methodology will be accentuated. And the purpose of the conversation becomes agendas. This will reflect in the writing of the stories, where life stories will resemble qualitative data clusters.

Notwithstanding the honest attempts made by the writers in most instances to sensitively evolve mutually-honouring relationship with the narrators, elements of patronage, expertise and inequality will still remain. It is quite likely that the process will tend to be extractive rather than mutually reflective, if proper orientation is not given to the story collectors to change the very structure of relationship.

Finally, the life stories written depends on the writing skills of the individual concerned and may end up not necessarily always reflecting the spirit of the conversation. In some instances where the stories are written in another language and translated into English, many of the idiomatic references about experiences and emotions needs to be ironed out.

Nonetheless the crucial outcome of the whole exercise is the acknowledgement on the part of those engaged in this exercise fully or otherwise about the extraordinary determining role that these conversations and life stories have the potential to play in both personal transformation as well as structural and methodological reflections – in perspective building, programme planning and institutional role definitions. Thus, while the drawbacks in the process are clear, so is the willingness to move further in overcoming them, as more and more of the process unfold. Many of the people involved in the project will learn to believe that such reflective processes ought to become the heart of many of the development practices undertaken by either individuals or institutions.

Documentation

Three forms of process documentation can be generated as part of the life story collection. The first are life stories themselves. The second is the analytical study on the specific issues chosen and the third is this study methodological refinements. All three will combine to produce a rich base of research information, insights and understandings about people who live in poverty, their specific contexts and the processes that underpin them. The individuals or institutions may further use the documentation pool to undertake work within their contexts, such advocacy work or to visibilise the conditions of the poor in media and have a commitment to creating life stories that can be used for advocacy.

Purpose

The very first is the purpose that such a study would serve. Given that the stories are to be representations of people who live in poverty in their own voices, the study would at best mediate their voices further. Such mediation could distort these voices as much as clarify them.

The World Bank had just released Voices of the Poor with a very detailed content analysis on the realities of people who live in poverty. The study at its very best seems to be a mere replication of the extensive work undertaken and the insights on poverty developed by the project team of the World Bank, notwithstanding the serious differences in perspective. Further, since listening to people in poverty is not conceived as a pure research project but as an action project, though it was to provide insights and understanding about poverty, study has to attempt reflecting the processual aspects of it. At the same time, it is essential to maintain rigour that a research document would carry in writing it so as to not render the whole exercise futile or worthless by having the integrity of the information contained questioned.

Guidelines

Let us first discuss the methods (actually attitudes and orientations) of life story selection and collection:

Selection

Intuitive selection of people to be jointly storied: The conventional research exercises assume a 'radical doubt' posture in a true modernist sense. This results in the chronic distrust and suspicion of the researcher and his/her motives and intentions. Thus the variety of dos and don'ts is aimed at dispelling the fear for potential dishonesty of the researcher. The researcher is enjoined to approach the research exercise in an unemotional way in the name of maintaining objectivity. There is a whole lot of literature available on the untenability of objectivity in social science research. Therefore we primarily believe in the essential honesty of the researcher and her commitment to the research endeavour. In the redefined research programme we propose, there is this honest mind of the researcher whose intuition is the only guide. The researcher, therefore, can choose the life story subject guided by her intuition, because the life story subject struck her powerfully or there is a hint for an intensity of the story in the life story subject or even any other intuitively triggered choices.

The successful stories are triumph of the personal relationship: It has to be kept in mind that the successful collection of the story is the product of an authentic personal relationship between the researcher and the life story subject. Even in the easiest of the circumstances where the story has been acquired easily because known people mediated such collection, it should still be asserted that the successful collection of story is the triumph of personal relationship. Though we may have to use the contacts already available to get to talk to the people, once we establish the contact with the people we should try to depend on our own personal strength to carry on the relationship when getting to collect their stories. We have to make all possible attempts to strike an authentic relationship as authentic persons.

Move from Group to Individuals: Instead of directly zeroing in on the individual life story subject it is better, wherever possible, to engage with the group first then move on to individual. We may have to meet and interact with many people who share similar experiences before we can select intuitively the one we write the story about. If we go by what the contact person says and select the case then there is no space for our intuition. Therefore it is better to move from groups to individuals.

If we have a choice let the people select themselves as we meet them in groups: We may have to recognize the basic freedom of the people to select themselves for the story. However it should not be because they are articulate or because they are able to silence others and dominate others. It should be a smooth process of selection in such a way that everyone agrees in a democratic manner to the person selecting oneself for the story to be told of her/him.

Collection

Abandon the expert in you: If we go as experts with all our sense of completeness and ability to be above all their problems them they may never feel free to tell the stories honestly. They may, at best, try to tell story in such a manner that it meets our expectations. Only if we present ourselves as one *like* them, in the sense of having limitations, problems and inadequacies (which all of us really *are*) then they may feel proximate to us.

Openness: Acknowledging the limitations of the listener to enter into the moral universe of the subject. We have to be honest about our limitations our inadequacies and tell that boldly to them. We the educated ones are clever in presenting a perfect image of ourselves despite all the ambiguities in us. Our ambiguities and dilemmas etc should be made evident to them so that they feel comfortable talking to us about their own ambiguities etc.

Demonstration of *havingbeenthereness*: As much as possible we have to recall incidences of humiliations, helplessness and powerlessness as well as the small victories and triumphs that happened in our own lives. The same must be shared without qualms. This will confirm that since we have been through these experiences we will be able to fully share their inner core.

Shift the burden of proving fitness in the research process and the emerging language from the subject to the listener: In conventional researchers it is the mostly the responsibility of the subjects (respondents) of the research to come out with answers that make sense to the research agenda, its hypothesis and variables. But actually it is the researcher's burden to meet the standards of the lived experiences of the people we study. If we aspire to study how people live their lives meaningfully then it is our burden to evolve a research design that captures the intensity of such life without distorting it. It means that we have to construct a research design that is extraordinarily sensitive to people's reality, rather than forcing the people's responses to measure up to the research design we have evolved.

The chronology of the subject's narration is more important. So we operate in their time and space. We never pull people to come to share their stories in times and places convenient to us. It should always be our going to their times and places convenient to the people whose stories we write. As much as possible we have to ensure that their life and the aspects about which we write stories do match in terms of times and space. For example if we wish to record their work life, wherever possible we may have to go to their work places. If it is about their families it would be ideal to meet them in their houses though not as a matter of compelling them to give permissions. Only if it happens naturally and unenforcedly should we do it, because it is very enriching to observe their life circumstances along with their descriptions of them.

Make it a multi-session interaction. Life story collection can never be a one-off exercise. Even in those circumstances where the life story subject opens oneself up fully thanks to the introduction provided by the contact person, it is imperative that we meet the subject for more than one interaction session. It always helps to meet them over two to three sessions so that we can go back, think intensely about them, and come back with more aspects to explore in the next sessions.

Making interview a retrospective remembrance. Since people's lives are too dynamic to be frozen in photographs and cassettes. And since listening to people is a humane exercise, we shall construct their stories with pure human strengths in us. This means that we will use our natural faculties in recording their stories rather than technological assistance. So as far as possible we can avoid intrusive devices such as voice recorder, note books, camera etc. Only when we are very sure of not distorting their life's intensity through the intervention of technical devises we should seek their assistance. Otherwise we can return and reflect on their lives after each session and prepare notes, rather than leaving the burden of engaging with such memories of intense interactions to the tapes of the cassettes or the films in the camera.

In the context of the life stories, we must understand that these stories when collating together should be able to produce a perspective for poverty. I presume that the theoretical framework and the methodological options have to be chosen by the stories themselves rather than the other way around. The stories having been written with the great deal of passion and regard for the storyteller, as a person capable of organizing her own life, thus, instead of fitting them into the frameworks we have a borrowed from faraway lands, we should ensure that the stories when pieced together select their own theoretical framework. This requires that we inform ourselves, as experts, of all the possible theoretical models that will help us to make sense of the stories.

It is very important that the researchers ensure an atmosphere that is characterized by an air of equality and democracy. When maintaining a conversation with the marginalized person it is crucial that we suspend our expert knowledge and present ourselves as a pure listening ear. It must be kept in mind that in the everyday situations a person has always shared her story not so much with an expert with whom they retain an element of suspicion or maintain a posture that is too ideal and perfect to believe. The more we present ourselves as a fellow traveler in a journey or as a bystander, the better they feel in sharing the stories with us.

Narrative isomorphism: This means that people always narrate their lives by narrating about other things they know. Maybe through the stories of flood, famine or village festival or even other persons they narrate about themselves. We should be sensitive to such layered narrations.Another aspect that has to be kept in mind is the popular habit often associated with humans to narrate their own stories when narrating others stories. This has been discovered by anthropologists who have studied folk songs as well as by other narrative analysts. They have found it too their amazement that into the stories and songs commonly available as part of the rural wisdom the narrator and the singer have woven their own personal stories either apparently or subtly. It is attributable to the creativity and imaginativeness of the people that they inscribe their own concerns into the narrations of public events and performances of the cultural items that are part of their customs and traditions. In the same token they insinuate their own stories even in the narration of public stories. The researchers have to be extremely sensitive to the personal stories that may lie buried in the public stories that they seemingly narrate. In a politically correct reversal of roles it is from the point of view of the researched that the researcher appears inadequate and acknowledges it at the first instance itself. The moral and the existential universe occupied by the research subjects can be grasped only participatively. It can be safely argued that the researchers are better off appearing as non experts who share the same existential universe rather than presenting themselves as experts.

Message in a Bottle: We always notice the situation in many places where the persons when talking to others would make it audible so that others to whom it may not have been addressed directly can hear it. For example the husband who talks to his wife in our presence would try to communicate his control over her and his own strengths and achievements through the way and things he speaks with her. The person who has passed his IAS examinations may want every one in the bus stop to know by loudly announcing to his friend but actually meaning it for others to hear. We may have to be mindful of such communications, which are basically messages in a bottle to reach any unknown or known receiver. In the story collection processes also one may come across such incidences where the narrator would float such messages in bottles that have to be captured by the researcher. Indeed in many instances we have found that the dignity-affirming narrations are not directly addressed to the researcher but in the form of a casual talk to their fellow-persons.

Allow people to correct their own statements: We may not have to correct the logical coherence in people's narrations. For example, if a sex worker talks about her age to be 35 but if we go by her narration of various stages in her life, should it amount to 45, then there is a plea for understanding her dilemma, rather logical correction. We may not need to correct it ourselves. Once trust is built she would confess to having given the incorrect information. But the burden to make her become comfortable with us lies on the listener researcher and her/his authentic relationship with the people.

<u>Writing the Analytical Document</u>

Finally, taking all these points into consideration, certain guidelines need to be worked out. The first is that the analytical document will provide a context to the stories rather than an analysis of the stories. Thus, it would be a larger narration that draws from the life stories and could act as a reference in reading them. By placing the study on the same narrative scale as the stories, I think that the perspective and the data of the study would be less of a superimposition and more of a parallel reflection to each of the stories. The second is that it would retain the process element at its core. Thus, the document would focus on the relational aspects within the stories rather than on the material or the data aspects. This focus I believe would allow us the freedom to prioritise emotions and experiences of the spirit. It would allow us to empathise with the stories and the people who narrated them by drawing out the commonalities in our human experiences. The third is to build the study through repeated readings of the stories. Thus, instead of breaking the stories into data units, we read them at as narrations to which we have intellectual and emotional responses.

The fourth and the most difficult is the framework. Given the complexity of the issue at hand, the different contexts of each of the stories and the expectations from the study, it is essential to evolve some sort of broad organising principle within the study. The decision to maintain human relations at the core needs to be clearly spelt out. Further the literature review on poverty must be worked out. In all these, relations between individuals and institutions ought to remain very significant. With each subsequent reading of the stories with these guidelines in mind, a framework of relations between people and institutions begins to evolve. This framework will be useful in contextualizing many of the common issues narrated in the stories, especially those over time. More importantly, it allows for reflection of processes over time, and the possibilities of change.

Having worked this out, the impulse to counter is the creation of categories and placing narrative segments into these categories. While these categories evolved from reading the stories, they nevertheless do not capture the layers of complexities that each story depicts. And we may find ourselves falling into the trap of content analysis and research goals and veering away from writing a process document. Further, the bias that pushes us to leans towards institutions rather than on the people whose stories are being recorded and their agency. Thus, the framework that originally evolved from the stories will begin to superimpose the stories and contour them. At this point, it must be decided to retain the framework as a guideline rather than the only organizing principle.

Reading the stories

The method of analyzing the life histories should express the very principles that life history as a method stands for. Though a very intuitive method of bringing the stories into some form of manageable data has to be adopted, we also need to ensure that such strategy does not miss out on the nuanced realities buried in the stories. Particularly the multi-layered nature of the rich insights and information and the inexhaustible qualitative data need to be mined from the stories for the purpose of substantiating arguments put forth. This is a complex task, for every time a story is read with different set of questions in mind, the same story fills us with a wealth of information on those questions. This means that there is no one final reading of the stories.

True to their nature, there is no single structure into which the stories can be straitjacketed. Similarly, there is no one single linear process along which the stories can be approached and subjected to analysis. Though there will be temptations to break the stories into manageable quantitative data, it will be against the very grain of life history methodology. By force of habit, we tend to value and build most of our arguments on the basis of those instances that are numerically abundant in the stories. This is a clear indication of quantification. Because here the focus is on the lookalike instances – only those insights that are similar in contours are taken to be overwhelming truths at the cost of the singular one-off insights that may hold more pathbreaking potency. Let me illustrate this by recalling a life story of sex worker: There is this instance in which the concerned individual talks about how as a sex worker she used reduced herself to a log of wood just to differentiate herself from being a bedfellow to her clients with being a wife to her husband. It is one such instance that may have come out in only one story but it is such as a powerful insight as to how poor people have been forced to reduce themselves to the status of objects and mere bodies – something that becoming the plight associated with the poor in globalisation time. Robert Chambers talks about one such instance in which he was struck by the statement found in a Participatory Poverty Assessment where he comes across the poor persons remarking that it is not lack of food that causes agony but the lack of dignity due to which the food consumed does not stick to the stomach.

Singular insights like these are very crucial for breaking new grounds in existing development wisdom. It has been my experience that most of what I have collected in the form of life histories required a re-reading of the same story from different points of view. This is done to ensure that one way of reading does not result in the missing out on other aspects in the same story. In other words, when we read the story from the point of view of the coping strategies that people evolve to counter the situations of powerlessness and poverty, we may miss out on the instances in which poverty would have overwhelmed them beyond redemption. Such manifestations of poverty need to be recorded in the same breath as the coping strategies. This requires a multilayered reading of the story, which means going back to the same story over and over again with the different questions in mind.

It has to be kept in mind that the stories, when collected properly, are very rich source of data for analysis and has to be treated as such. The richness of people's lives depicted there must be retained without reducing them to teased-out quotations and fragmented pieces that are chosen simply because they dovetail with our framework of understanding. Instead the stories have to be kept as touchstones against which the merit of the frameworks evolved have to be rubbed. It is not that the stories have to fit in with the frameworks but it is the frameworks that have to fit in with the stories. At least the ability of the frameworks to hold against challenges posed by the stories has to be constantly tested.

Indeed, that is what we need to do in our analysis of stories in the process of analyzing them. We read the stories treating them mostly as finished works of art that can hold themselves on their own when it comes to narrating the experiences of poverty. Yet they can also present themselves as data that can lend themselves for analysis. The first aspect helps us to read the stories without losing the passion and the human elements that are essential for giving the understanding of poverty a human face. We went about reading the stories in their fullness to get a feel of the poverty experiences of the people whose lives we have documented. This helped us to capture the human aspects of the poverty and their manifestations without fracturing them into pieces of data or information.

One solution comes in the form of treating the stories as stories as objects and stories in contexts. This offers the way out in the form of making the stories as works of art as well as pieces of data. When we work with as objects we shall be able to treat them significantly.

An important component is on how the stories will be read. The overwhelming impulse in us is to read the stories as chunks of qualitative data and to subject them to content analysis. The very richness in each story may further this impulse. But the very richness of the stories poses both ethical and practical challenges. There is this perennial dilemma in us as to whether to treat lifehistories as mere pieces of data or to treat them as finished works that on theirs own speak of the impoverished people's social realities. We may be tempted to leaving the lifehistories as such to reflect the poverty situations of people without subjecting themselves to any degree of abstraction or extraction.

As a way out we may adopt a two-stage reading of the lifehistories. Essentially, we all agree that the stories, though amenable to derivation of insights, are finished works of art in their own right. Thus, we largely read the stories as what they essentially are, namely, comprehensive account of human lives. A thorough reading of the stories with a passion, intensity and open mindedness, with which we normally approach any finished work of art, permitted us to see and sense significantly overarching experiences and dimensions of poverty. Certain gross reductions, emotions, anguishes and triumphant demonstration of meaning-making, coping and humanity-affirming acts will strike us very forcefully. We simply will have to be mindful of these and enumerate our reflection on these stories *in retrospect* and compare and crosscheck our responses among us to look for the patterns of experiences and impact of poverty in individual stories.

However, in the first stage of reading we need not just look for dominant patterns or numerically preponderant instances only. Indeed, doing so would unjustly relegate one-off facts and acts found in the lifehistories as mere aberrations. Contrarily, we may recall even those singular facts and acts and treated them as holding possibilities of even fulfilling quantitative criterion of numerical massiveness, if we expand the universe and range from which lifehistories are collected. Besides this quantitative mandate, we ought to hold our selves ethically responsible to treat even singular events as capable of repeating themselves on all humanity if unchecked (in those cases of disastrous experiences) or if consciously promoted (in those cases of empowering experiences).

From this we need to move on to the second stage, which involves several laps of reading the individual stories with the clear purpose of evidence-collection. In the process of completing this stage of reading, where stories are regarded as stories-as-data, we will have to subject the stories to multi-layered reading. In other words, endowed with an understanding as to what aspects to look for in each story, we will have to go back to reading the collected stories many times over. To put it arithmetically, if we have four themes to guide us, say, 1. reduction of poor to labouring-bodies, 2. institutional impoverishment, 3. their dignity-affirming acts and 4. poor's understanding of redemption, then stories will be read four times over. This will effectively be equal to reading 1000 stories.

This we need to do principally to avoid missing out on one aspect of life-in-poverty, when looking for another aspect. However, for all practical purposes the stories will have to be read more times than even the figure we cited above, since certain singular insights found in one story will impel us to look for the same in several other stories. This in my experience is the best way to pay tribute to the intensity of lives lived by the poor in the stories. It is also way of confirming and demonstrating our commitment to treat the stories-as-artworks in their own right.

Conclusion

Life story collection is much more than a research method. It is an attitude of mind, a disposition of heart. In the prevailing circumstances where the conventional research behavioral traits dominate, promoting, leave alone institutionalizing, life story method is bound to be an incomplete task for some time to come. Since this method calls for radical rediscovery of forgotten attitudes and bends of mind (among which listening is the most crucial) – forgotten because scientifically designed research did not permit them to surface – many of the stories collected and presented here in the following pages still suffer from some limitations, despite the best efforts of the researchers. For many, life story collection may still stand as a method rather than a value and orientation of heart. However, by privileging this method of collecting data, we have given legitimacy and significance to different ways of being a researcher and a person. Soon the alternative ways of doing research may come to complement other conventional ways, and hopefully create a radically new development researcher in the nearest future.

Notes and References

[*] The choice of the word itself smacks of the arrogance of behavioural psychology which coined the word in fact. The 'respondents' have as much freedom only to respond to the stimuli from the scientist researcher, as the rats and other hapless animals had in the researches conducted in highly controlled environments. Instead of responding, if the researched being acts on its own, it would make no sense to the researcher or it would invite punishment, in the true behavioural psychological sense.

[**] See the following two essays for a very detailed discussion on how humans lead storiyable lives: *Autoethnography, Personal Narrative,Reflexivity Researcher as Subject* by Gery W Ryan and H Russell Bernard and *Life History*

and the Postmodern Challenge by John Beverley, in Norman K. Denzin and Yvonna S. Lincoln. (March 2000) *Handbook of Qualitative Research*, Sage Publications

$ Consider these statements by Mills, "The sociological imagination enables us to grasp history and biography and the relations between the two within society. That is its task and its promise. ... No social study that does not come back to the problems of biography, of history and of their intersections within a society has completed its intellectual journey."

[1] See Jean Dreze's note "On Research and Action", in *Economic and Political Weekly*, March 02, 2002

[2] In choosing impoverishment over poverty, we are fully with Upendra Baxi. His anger with the term poverty is explained in the introduction to the book *Law and Poverty: Critical Essays* (1998)

3 In fact the World Development Report 2001 was titled "Attacking Poverty". In this context it is instructive to note that Robert Chambers (2001, p.306) advocated, in true appreciation of the right strategy for eliminating poverty, that at least WDR 2010 be titled, "Challenging Wealth and Power"

IV

Where Heart Rules Head! Some Observations on Social Research

Social research of most kinds essentially has to deal with human experiences in their original forms, as they obtain in social contexts. Though we may rely on documents and texts that have recorded human experiences, an authentic social research is done when it deals with human experiences directly, what with, social, in a true Weberian sense, essentially meaning 'orientation to others'. The social research remains social only to the extent that it seeks to concern itself with human social experiences.

Once we set upon ourselves the task of studying human experiences, it is incumbent upon us to refrain from engaging in mere collection of information. Specially, one has to bear in mind the changed background in which there is this refreshing understanding that any social research cannot be a mere fact-gathering exercise, but a demonstration of our social responsibility and commitment to social change, as there is a consciously made choice to study the people we focus our research on. Thus, social research is a social responsibility exercise and consequently the methods we choose to apply ought to be relationship methods.

In the social research we do, there can only be points of entry – the points at which we, as researchers make the momentous decision to responsibly relate to the people we study. There are no exit points, much as we cannot have exit points from many of the relationships we have been born with – like our relationships as children to our parents, as parents to our children or between siblings etc.

This is because, social research no longer needs to be conducted in the orthodox sense of researchers comfortably walled by notions of objectivity and expertise. The wall has collapsed, as it were. If social research is a relationship exercise, then researchers have to relate to the subject of the research on equal footing. In other words, our attempts to explore the experiential universe of the homeless people cannot happen without the active cooperation of the people themselves. In our endeavours to reconstruct the lived-reality of the social actors, the people are primary authors, as they continue to experience the reality much before we attempt to study them. Hence, we have to recognize co-authorship of the people we study in the research project. In this sense they are co-researchers, if we are core-researchers. In the remaining pages of this essay we cease to use the word "subjects" to refer to 'respondents', in its stead we use the word co-researchers.

The 'subjects' of the research have to become "co-researchers" for a variety of reasons as indicated below:

1. In most of the orthodox quantitative research exercises, it is the intentions of the researchers that dominate the research agenda, rather than the 'intentions' of the co-researchers. Given the options, the co-researchers would have shared what makes immediate sense and what holds deep relevance to their lives, rather than merely respond to that of researcher. In our research, we have to effect a non-conflictual interplay of intentions of researchers and co-researchers. To achieve this, we have to imagine the very research exercise as that which *generates right and enabling human/social processes*, rather than that which limits itself to *asking right questions*. **Essentially, social research is not about asking right questions but is about allowing right processes to emerge.**

2. In much of the conventional research projects, the researchers expect deeply-felt and authentic answers and information from the co-researchers, even while the researchers aspire to remain authentic *only* to their research design and its structure, rather than to the co-researchers. In other words, while the researchers want the co-

researches to speak from their hearts, the researchers themselves remain cerebral as they are busy remembering sequences and structured answers.

3. In our radical understanding of social research, we have to permit a creative and authentic union of heart-to-heart dialogues and conversations, by turning the researchers into feeling and acting persons, rather than as thinking persons. Foundationally, social research cannot be subject-object interaction, but a subject-to-subject dialogue.

This necessitates immersion in the experiences we wish to explore in the company of co-researchers. All the research questions, if ought to emanate from the hearts of the researchers, have to be internalized in such a manner that they haunt the heart/mind of the researcher. Internalization has to happen in the form of imaginatively living and feeling the questions along with co-researchers. This cannot happen if the living universes of the researchers and co-researchers are thought to remain separated and irreconcilable. The researcher has to give up the outsider positions with reference to the universe he/she explores, but should imaginatively immerse in the universe he/she enquires into.

Thus, the mechanical reproduction and reciting of questions will not have the right to elicit sensitive answers from the co-researchers. The questions have to transform into haunting issues that have a life of their own, as well as a form and intensity perfectly approximate to the inquisitiveness of the reflective members among the co-researchers. Put it differently, the researchers have to carry these questions in the heart and ask them in the manner in which one homeless would ask the other -- not so much in the manner of getting answers, but also collectively searching for them. It is here that social research turns into an illuminating humanist exercises, leadings both the researcher and co-researcher to a position of critical-self-awareness or critical subjectivity.

Social Research as Action Research

Social research is not only about human experiences and relationship of equality it presupposes between the research and co-researchers, but also an action research. But in reality, much of the research endeavours, by resorting to terminological feat and sleight of hand, such as preservation of objectivity, rigorous quantification and vast coverage, characterize themselves as pure research. In the realm of human experience, no research can claim to pure information-gathering agenda without touching the lives of people it purports to study. Even the most rigorously quantitative studies aiming only to collect observable data from the human persons, tend to generate expectations, promises and disappointments from the people it studies. In several other cases such studies tend to 'spoil the field' for the subsequent researchers, thanks to the badly established relationships with the people. These may all happen, despite the studied objectivity and detachment of the researchers.

But in social research of the kind we propose, not only the co-researchers end up undergoing changes – changes of expectations, or self-awareness – but, also the researchers, who give up the impossible objectivity for the sake of critical subjectivity. Quite apart from the mutual transformation that a qualitatively oriented social research causes in the primary actors of social research, such research needs also to presume and eventually lead to a broader social change through expression of responsibility and solidarity between the researchers and co-researchers. It is in this sense, that we visualize the social research as an action research.

The community of core-researchers and co-researchers is characterized by its consistency of involvement across the length of study and the subsequent programmatic interventions. The community of researchers also operates along shared-conscience basis. If the researchers are primarily triggered by the passion to touch the lives of the homeless people positively, such passion must be passed on to and generated in the co-researchers too. This produces a heightened commitment and responsibility. It also creates moral accountability to each other. It goes without saying, that there is no limit of the membership in this community of researchers who can agree to share the conscience of the others who are already citizens of the community.

The community of action researchers, as previously stated, firmly believes that research is primarily a relationship exercises characterized by generation of right processes, rather than by conjuring up right questions. Thus, they aspire to involve in the life-worlds of the select people's lives and the community, and its moral universes as authentic individuals. Getting right answers can only happen as an outcome of attitudinal transformation and authentic immersion. Once an authentic relationship evolves through mutual transparency, then raw fact-gathering can happen more as a voluntary disclosure or even as an expression of trust.

Embodying the Questions

In conventional research, the researchers carry the questions in such a generalized manner, that they are disembodied enough not to present the images of persons. In this sense they are like the quantified data that erase the thinking and feeling human persons from face of their numerical figures. What remain are absolutely disembodied data, emptied of the soul, blood and flesh, they seek to stand for. In conventional social research, even the highly descriptive statements of human experiences and social reality are vested with the same fate befalling the quantified numerical data. These descriptive statements are bereft of the soul and alive beings they speak of. This is because of over-generalization that social research of the conventional kind aims to achieve.

This has its origin also in the way research inquiry is conducted. On close scrutiny, one finds that in conventional social research, not only the disembodied generalizations are converted into queries, but they are also fractured to the extent of not approximating to the life worlds of the people it studies. Societies and people evolve in such a manner as to experience a sense of wholeness and wholesomeness. There is an observable pattern and mosaic noticed even by the common-sense perception. Our enquiries into the lives of people and the societies they live have to preserve such mosaic when proceeding and evolving from one question/issue to another. If we fail, we would end up fracturing their experiential universe beyond recognition for them.

Hence, we have to take immense care to embody our queries in the feeling, living human persons and feel them in the same way co-researchers themselves are experiencing the agony, joy and anguish of issues we explore. In the same manner we have to essentially evolve our enquiries in the way the co-researchers may have evolved and pieced themselves together in their real lives.

Ethics

We have to remember that what we aspire suggest here is explicitly action research, through all social research exercises are action research, willy-nilly. Thus, in the process of entering into the moral universe of the co-researchers and their life-worlds, and listening to them, we may end up touching their lives. We make all efforts to touch their lives positively, as we wish to ensure that they too touch our lives positively. Our authentic relationship and collective sensing of reality may help all of us – researchers and co-researchers - to change, modify and alter our conception of our 'selves' and our reality. We should be cautious enough to lead such transformation to affect critical self-awareness for empowerment, and conscientisation along mutual lines, and not as a one-way process.

Care must be taken to remain non-judgemental; care must also be taken not to promise what we cannot deliver. The best we can offer is each other's friendship and any positive effects that can follow from it.

Social research deals with 'real' people, not their texts and recorded speeches. Hence we must pay close attention to their hopes, aspirations, feelings and dynamics of relationships, so as not to cause backlashes, social breakdowns and mutual animosity. At every stage we must be sensitive to the aftermath of the research, unlike in other one-off or even conventional research endeavours where the researchers are least bothered about the aftermath of the research, as they reel out promises and leave the stage after the research to others.

As stated elsewhere we have to work with people with whom we envisage a long-term engagement beyond research. Let us not engage with the community or groups only for the extractive purpose of fact-gathering. Let us not spoil the field for the next phase of the research.

V

Gandhi, Poverty Studies and Social sciences

Poverty studies in all their manifestations are seemingly immune to the critical inputs from social sciences, particularly the post-modern and Gandhian visions. Pitching their significance only in relation to policy influencing and policy making, they sacrifice research rigour and critical inquiry for the sake of arriving at spectacularly grand generalizations that are amenable to policy formulations. In the same spirit, they seldom engage in a self-reflexive inquiry into their own ways of constructing the categories that are now taken as 'given', for example 'poverty' as a construct. Since their very existence and relevance rest on postulating a foundational reality called 'poverty', they present it as a well-rounded singular object and as an ever-persisting reality.

The present research should be sensitive to this lacuna in poverty studies. Even though it is not our primary purpose in our endeavour here to elaborate on the benefits of reflexive exercise in the research we are carrying out, we should remain tempered by the spirit of reflexive inquiry throughout research exercise.

Even in the research we propose to undertake we wish to grab such an opportunity to bring in the insights offered by social sciences, particularly anthropology with both tempered by eastern world view. It is only in the light of such world-view we realize that poverty studies have never benefited from an intense ethnographic research on the poverty experiences of individuals. Much of the participatory approaches within Development

Studies are short-term engagement with acquiring people's perception on poverty. It is incumbent upon development research to complement the survey-based and PRA-based poverty research with ethnographic research. This not only has high degree of intellectual value but also political value, since the later concerns the politics of poverty research. The inferences we can make from anthropological ethnographic research tell us many striking things about what is absent and overly present in poverty studies, though it may be instructive to remember that Social sciences including anthropology are not overtly concerned about poverty for reasons delineated below. Therefore, asking poverty studies to behave like social sciences is not only overambitious but even questionable. However, there are certain tendencies in social sciences that have to be emulated in poverty studies as much as there are certain practices and conceptual shortcuts in poverty studies that have to be abandoned. Indeed the problems of poverty studies become more glaring only in the light of the spirit of reflexivity that so wonderfully characterizes social sciences. Thus, we are going to benefit immensely by knowing why poverty is not studied by social sciences with the same intensity as poverty studies, as much as by the awareness as to why poverty studies do it obsessively.

However, with the arrival of post-structuralist approach to social reality, which is seen as a construct, poverty too is being viewed as a construct with political and ideological underpinnings. Once again it is through extrapolation that we come to such understanding. But inquiring directly into poverty as a social construct is few. One among them is Majid Rahmema, who argues, "Global poverty is an entirely new and modern construct. The basic materials which have gone into the construct are essentially the economization of life and the forceful integrations of vernacular societies into the world economy."

Once poverty is understood as a 'construct', the deconstruction of it leads to the reinvention of human as free individuals, who do not define themselves in terms of lack and deficiency. Such is the power of this construct that by successfully amalgamating local conditions of absence of material wealth with the global conception of material wealth as the necessary and sufficient condition of good life, the social majority of humanity has been reduced to non-humans in need of assistance. What is worse, instilling that sense of such social majority, it has made "seeking assistance" as part of their self-definition. When the non-rich (materially) believes that they are 'poor' and only through external assistance they can overcome their being poor, what gets valorized is the whole army of development experts and their institutional apparatuses-they alone can eradicate poverty.

What the development studies has done, or what the mainstream social sciences has failed to question, is absolutisation of 'poverty' as material deficiency. While material deficiency was definitely part of people's expectation of distress and destitution in the pre-modern societies they were deeply embedded in their culture and linked to spatial-temporal specialties.

How each culture or even each category of people went about constituting non-materiality, differed from one society to another or even within a society. In a similar manner, a whole host of non-material aspects too were considered as constituting destitution. This non-materiality too was culturally embedded. In some cultures, not having neighbours to live close-by gave them a sense of deficiency, whereas in certain other societies and groups having too many neighbours living in close proximity was distressing. Besides these, other culturally deemed notion too come to define inability, such as abandonment, not having people to love and be loved, neglect, not having respect, domination by others, discrimination, oppression, deprivation, hunger, malnutrition, homelessness ill-health and exclusion from educational possibilities etc had been considered as constituting their experience of "meaningless-ness".

The deconstruction of poverty will also lead to rescue of human from a whole gamut of reductionism to which he/she has been subjected to. It may also result in the triumph of local versus the global, because, at present, the latter seems to have imposed its abstraction on the lived experience of the vernacular societies.

We argue that it can rescue human, because, the existing discourse on poverty has devalued human beings as meaning-seeking individuals and indeed reduced them as salable commodities through the notion of labour-as-essence, as in the same way as the earth has become a saleable product through the notion of land. What it has entailed is that the poor is one who in unable to sell himself/herself to meet his/her requirements.

The equation of man with labour and nature with land has its origin in the economization of society, whereby resourcelessness came to be defined as a problem. And resourcefulness acquired extraordinary significance. Therefore, economic resourcefulness largely in the form of material resources became identified with being 'developed' and the lack or absence of which is being 'underdeveloped'. It gets further individualized when such resourcefulness is equated with personal possessions. Those without individual possessions in abundance need to emulate the ones with lots of such individual possessions.

In this scheme of things what is available to the community or group as a whole does not qualify the members of such group or community as 'resourceful' people. For instance as individual with unusual quantity of wealth even in the midst of the community of people suffering from hunger or malnutrition or oppressions and dominations is still wealthy, whereas the eastern worldview before being influenced by modernity saw meaninglessness not at the individual level but at the collective community level. The suffering of one's community or another member thereof is also the suffering of the evaluating individual. The state of existence of any of his/her caste member is also extended upon the evaluating individual of the same caste.

Even today in many villages in Tamil Nadu, when a family loses a member the grief is shared collectively in such a way that the whole village mourns it by avoiding loud music and other celebrations. Similarly, the wealth of one member is also the wealth of the entire community. Even today one can hear a resourceless individual of a village, feeling proud of the big house in his village, even though the big house does not belong to him/her. In such societies the individual self-definition is deeply embedded in the self-definition of the community as a whole. I remember some of my friends who when taking me to their village, proudly showing me big houses, while feeling ashamed when guiding me around sewage waters running helter-skelter around the streets.

But what modern/capitalistic logic has done is to subjugate the collective consciousness to quantified individualized global abstractions. In the same way, the cultural understanding of self gets subordinated to the economic understanding of self. This consequently has led to subjugation of local by national and even more dangerously of national by global. What emerged from such series of subjugations is that materiality has got triumphed over non-materiality.

The death of diversity in understanding one's existence occurs exactly at the point when singular global-level abstract definition of poverty is imposed on the psyche of everyone. Thus, in contrast to societies that valued detachment over attachment to material possessions, "having more" material wealth come to be privileged. In place of societies that united individual with communities when defining their selves, releasing of the individuals from the holds of the communities got prioritized. The reversal of hierarchies ended up privileging a whole host of development experts who can be trained only in western/modern knowledge system. Similarly, the right to judge whether some one is poor has been divested from concerned individuals or their communities and has got vested in global institutional apparatuses located in western world. Curiously these institutions are the creations of the western nations that privilege themselves only on account of possessing more material wealth, though concentrated in the individual hands.

Here once sees a curious paradox: While the western world treats the unusual wealth of one individual/individuals as generalizable to the healthiness of their societies, they refuse to generalize the wealth/ resourcefulness of the society or communities to the individuals in the eastern societies or the impoverished in their own societies. This paradox is sustained only because wealth is quantified in the form of GDPs and per-capita incomes, rather than seen as an experience whose quality and necessity is left to the assessment and judgment of individuals/ communities. It is true that the so-called rich nations like USA has vast oceans of improvised people, yet the country remains a rich nation. If one goes by Mandela's understanding of freedom or Gandhian understanding of liberation, then the so called rich nations will have to lose all their moral authorities to judge other humanities as 'poor'. Mandela in one of the profound statements he has made says "Freedom is indivisible; the chains on any one of my people were the chains on all of them, the chains on all of my people were the chains on me". Gandhi in his own refreshing way says that the dawn of freedom will not occur if the last man in India is not liberated. And it is a public knowledge that Gandhi refused to enjoy any luxuries of the world, until such luxuries reached the last man on the earth.

But such sense of shame and guilt has been made to vapourize with the arrival of experts and expert institutions on the one hand and compartmentalization of individual psyche as conterminous to individual body and experience on the other. The very moment of acceptance of oneself as resourceful, is also the very moment at which the moral responsibility and joint humanity with the existence of the other get dispelled from the vision.

In this effort the role of social sciences is decisive. Particularly the science of psychology has contributed immensely to the atomization of individual mind, by inventing such compartmentalized psyche as emerging and dying with the birth and death of such individual.

In Gandhian and Buddhist view of poverty on can see the tendency to culturalise and moralize poverty in contrast to the overly secularized and abstracted conception of poverty enunciated by western paradigms. In social science framework too such culturalised understanding of poverty was absent until the arrival of Amartya Sen–whose eastern sensibilities aiding that cannot be exaggerated.

The strength of Gandhian vision is that the cultural context of poverty is called into question rather than mere condition of poverty. In such a vision one avoids the tragic tendency of locating poverty in the poor -- his/her lack of initiative and effort. In the secularized understanding of poverty, not only the poverty of the individual is traced to the individual psyche, but even the poverty of the entire society gets traced to the individual poor. It is through this unfair tracing the poor gets solidified into a group, though they themselves are a highly variegated people in their own right. But this location of poverty in poor becomes necessary for the experts to rescue themselves as the cause of poverty.

But, by locating poverty in the cultural context and seeing it as the product of the prevailing structure of unequal relationship, Gandhian vision calls into question the issue of dominance, oppression and inequality in power and conceptual categories organized in favour of the most powerful. Thus, poverty is seen as the outcome of conceptual shifts as well as the result of relationship patterns. Here the blame is laid at the doorsteps of knowledge producers and dominant groups.

But this uncomfortable vision must be laid to rest and put to relegation. As new scapegoat has to be found so that the 'resourceful' group can exonerate itself, it becomes all the more necessary to locate the scapegoat that has 'frustrated' every well-meaning attempt at development. Excluded a priori were those experts that had prepared or advised the general strategies for the eradication of poverty. On the other hand it was equally embarrassing to accuse the intellectually bankrupt governments of most of the southern nations for the continued troubled state of affairs.

Those left open that final, easily available common target for the abuses of despair - the low-income groups, including the landless labourer the small farmer, the unemployed craftsman. And since they could be calculated upon not to react or return the attack, experts and government set about the task at will.

But what is forgotten and swept under the carpet is the truth that "the principal obstacles set in the path of the emancipation of the poor came not from below but from above -- from the ruling groups at the village, regional, national and international levels, who only allowed change on their own terms".

In the Gandhian vision we can note the problematisation of, both material and culture of wealth-making as the cause of poverty, rather than poor. It is immensely significant to remember that when Gandhi talks of trusteeship, he lists out prescription for the so called 'resourceful' to re-vision their wealth-making and their relationship with wealth. Throughout his writing/thinking he formulated lessons for the rich and other resourceful groups change their ways of being.

In sum Gandhi provides enough scope for the social origins of poverty and clearly argues that poverty as scarcity as socially-produced rather than as objectively existing.

VI
Studying Poverty: Evolving a Framework

Introduction

Humans are always in the process of 'becoming'. To define them in terms of what they are *now* is like defining the stream as a handful of static, non-flowing water at the time of scooping it into our hands. In the social universes that people occupy, this continuous process of 'becoming' is not, by necessity, in one singular direction, characterized by the prevailing wisdom as a forward moment, with all the positive connotations attached to it namely betterment, growth, improvement and development. People in society are multi-directionally 'becoming'.

Individuals occupy various points of intersections where several social forces meet and converge. In this, they are 'becoming' rich from 'being' poor, 'becoming' poor from 'being' economically better-off, 'becoming' poorer from 'being' poor and so on and so forth (Baulch and McCulloc, 1998). This swirl of human 'becoming' is becoming pulled in two directions under the influence of dualistic modern processes. There are a vast majority of people in the globe only who 'become' poorer from 'being' poor across generations, years, months and even days. Simultaneously, there is a significant *minority* 'becoming' richer from being rich on an *everyday* basis (Narayan et al, 2000a & 2000b). And there are those who are amongst the poorest, who remain frozen in time and excluded from becoming. These experience human processes with all its crushing intensity across all the three grammatical divisions of time, viz., past present and future and are trapped always in the immediate.

This chapter attempts to evolve a framework that captures the various processes that structure a particular way of 'becoming' of individuals in Asia – 'being' poor to 'becoming' poorer, and perpetuate a particular way of 'being', namely, the poorest, who are congealed in poverty forever and caught in some sort of a time warp, as it were. The framework thus formulated here is only indicative and not exhaustive. It aspires to capture the predominant tendencies observable in the lives of the people, selected for the Listening to People in Poverty Project. In this sense it is very specific to the experiences narrated in the whole array of stories.

In understanding the various impoverishing processes, it is imperative that we spell out our understanding of poverty here and the key concepts used in evolving the framework.

Poverty as causal and symptomatic

The departure aginst the dominant understanding of poverty was made when we read the life histories of the people closely. The life histories critically challenge the belief that lack of resources causes human distress and death. While it is true that lack of resources does exacerbate distress people face, it is symptomatic (Michael and Nunn, 1994) of the relations that people have, and the extent to which they can value, access, control and negotiate resources within these relations. Thus agency – the ability of the individual to create and maintain relations of their own volition – becomes central to addressing poverty issues. These life stories emphatically place the cause of their distress in the decimation of their agency in accessing and controlling resources, and the kind of relations within which this decimation occurs. Attacks on poverty therefore are merely attacks on the symptoms of the global malaise and not on the causes that created the malaise. Much of the solutions focussing on merely attacking lack of money are therefore also symptomatic. These reflections and solutions tend to provide short-term relief rather than long-term transformation.

Impoverishment is therefore the consequence of disempowering people by depleting their physical energies and devaluing their knowledge; and by constricting their access and control to resources, by rendering useless the resources they already possess or by denying their traditional access to natural / common resources (EPW, 2000). This ensures that people can be controlled and directed by powerful interests to maintain inequitable distribution and for individual profit. These processes are created through relations that deny the ability of people to participate and own the institutions that operate in their lives and value the resources that they have access and control to within their social and economic transactions. Impoverishing processes are authored and maintained by powerful institutions and are translated into day to day relationships that disempowered people are forced to have.

Individuals and institutions interact through relationships. If the majority of these relationships are exploitative or contractual rather than affirmative, it eventually leads to distress, disempowerment and impoverishment. Ultimately for a world that is free from poverty, there is need for not merely symtomatic relief but of individual, personal and societal transformation – one that is based on honest reflections on the kind of relations that each human being creates. One that is able to see the kinds of relations that are predominant today, and the effects of these relations and a push towards transformations into better forms of relating. This then would open the possibilities of creating realities where it does not become necessary to disempower or impoverish many to fatten a few.

Poverty as uni-dimensional and Poverty as multi-dimensional

With modernisation, resources have been homogenised into numbers. Thus complex resources that people control and access when homogenised into their monetary income offers no insights into processes that disempower people, limit their agency and therefore impoverish them. In real life, people use resources that they have access to and control in multiple ways in order to negotiate their environment. In order to understand impoverishment, the idea of money has to be unpacked into the resources it has come to represent in a monetised world (Hart, 1999). Thus the economic well-being of a person is closely related to their control of different kinds of resources related to knowledge, time and space. For a person to make choices that allow her to negotiate her life freely, she must have knowledge about the various actors and their institutions that affect her life, the time to reflect on her/his past experiences, the knowledge and skills that are useful to her/him and the space to feel capable of living these choices. These resources are evaluated by exploitative and powerful interests and their institutions, homogenised and monetised so as to allow their accumulation by individual interests. Thus indigenous knowledge, metis, physical labour, reproductive labour, time and many other resources are all reduced into purely monetary, contractual exchanges, trivialised and underpaid.

In daily transactions, impoverishment is due to the depletion of the bodily resources and devaluation of metis - knowledge acquired through praxis and is based on intensive local understanding with the environment which people have traditionally used to surive. Under the reduced circumstances, people who live in poverty are compelled by immediate necessities to operate in the present, leaving no oppurtunity to reflect on the past and to plan for the future. The space allowed for privacy, movement and transaction constricted by different institutions within which the person operates.

Poverty as individual experience and Poverty as a collective experience

The third is the process of compartmentalisingi and individualising impoverishment – blaming the victim. Thus, economic well-being is seen as a consequence of individual merit and capacities (sometimes accumulated in previous lives through *karma!*). These processes reflect on the experiences and realities of the disempowered as if the phenomenon occurs independently of the lives and experiences of the powerful. Social institutions controlled by powerful stakeholders that author larger processes within which an individual acts escape scrutiny and reflection. Thus, they do not have to be accountable for their actions and change. Simultaneously, attempts to 'eradicate' poverty augment the process of individualisation by reducing impoverished people to mere welfare beneficiaries.

The third insight relates to the need for structural transformation that is located in the reality of individual experience and her relations and transcends into the structures and processes that these individuals create or forced to be part of. Thus reflections about poverty cannot happen in isolation, independent of the values of the society and world in large and the translation into institutions and processes that the individual operates within. Unless the values of reflection, of mutual dignity, justice and non-violence are encoded in the larger social institutions, the state and the global forces, unless there is transformation within the larger power structures – merely expecting this reflection within the poor person places undue pressures of change on people who are already burdened by survival.

A Framework for Understanding Impoverishing Processes

In the backdrop of this, the reading of the life histories of the people living in poverty entailed a thorough and deep reflection on the voices of the people, the variety of processes affecting them and the strategies and solutions evolved by them to overcome them. This provided data about poverty as well as understanding about the causes for their impoverishment. The central question in the reflection process was: how can the fundamental rights of the most vulnerable to their violation within the human society can protected? The related questions were: who is excluded from accessing means to realise their rights? What are the structures and processes that exclude people from accessing resources needed to exercise their rights? Why and how does this exclusion occur? Who benefits? How do people forced to live without freedom and dignity endure it? what is the nature of agency that people who have lived in poverty have? How can the transformation of human structures and processes be directed so as to ensure that the rights of the all people can be protected?

This reflection on poverty focusses on the relations that people living in poverty are forced or choose to have with the current structures and processes. It is structured around the agency of the people, the institutions that they are forced / choose to live within and the relations between the two.

Agency is the ability of the individual to express herself freely as long as it does not harm others and is able to create and maintain relations of her own volition. It allows her to determine the value of the resources she accesses and controls in transactions within these relations; and to access resources that is essential for her self-expression and creativity when she wishes to. It is the extent to which she is able to be autonomous – to create, own and transform institutions that she belongs to, is able to regulate herself and is able to seek justice for violations of her freedoms and person. Underpinning the notion of personal agency is the recognition of the diversity that exist in the human experience and expression. (Giddens, A, 1984).

Institutions form the web of relations within which the individual exerts her agency. Institutions are both formal and informal structures that have definite values and rules operationalised through structures and processes (WDR, 2001/2002). Thus, insitutions depend on the values of inclusion and exclusion that they acknowledge and operationalise. The orientation of the institution depend on its positions and values along different axes: the extent to which the institution supports its members to freely express themselves and make their life choices; recognition and negotiation of difference and dissent within the institutional collective; the degree of equity in the distribution of knowledge and other resources; the extent of effectivity and inclusion of justice and grievance redressal mechanisms; the ability to self-reflect honestly and transform through the process.

The life stories of people who live in poverty offer the possibility of a different framework of reflection. This framework holds that in order to understand poverty, it is essential to understand the kinds of the relations that people who live in poverty are forced to have. The categories outlined are indicative, and not comprehensive. As human relations and processes are multi-layered, complex interactions cannot be completely represented through any single framework. Given this, this framework merely aims to look at one set of possible interactions between the individual and the institutions that she is embedded within.

Institutional Orientation

Institutions are both formal and informal structures that have definite values and rules operationalised through structures and processes (WDR, 2001/2002). Three kinds of institutions have been outlined here based the way they exist and operate.

Institutional orientation	Kind of relation	Agency
Traditional	Exploitative	Compelled
Modern	Contractual	Surviving
Affirmative	Constructive	Creative

Figure 1. Instituional Orientation

Exploitative Institutions

These institutions are premised on threat, survival and maintanenance of status quo. They value their members differentially based on differences of birth, culture and resources, and place importance on the survival of its most powerful 'important' members. They emphasise punitiveness to ensure that their members conform to their norms and rules.

These institutions acknowledge and hierarchalise differences thus creating discriminatory, marginilising and excluding patterns of interaction. They also hierarchialise information and forms of knowing, and prevent most of their members from accessing the 'higher' forms of knowing, while devalueing their own knowledge. Individual and collective expression is seen as possible sources of dissent and threatening status quo and therefore is silenced/punished or labeled irrelevant. They compel their members into actions that prove inimical to their interests and survival. They distribute resources based on discriminatory/marginal positions. The discriminatory practices are encoded in the justice systems ensuring that there is no recourse to justice, beyond the boundaries laid down by them. Those who move or are pushed beyond these boundaries are not protected and/or punished. The system is owned by a few and influences or forces other members to work in the interests of those few. The self-reflection of these institutions is usually a mere documentation of their own achievements and do not include the experiences of all their members. The concern for the future is restricted to merely the survival of those who are powerholders within the institution. Many of them have a long existence historically and have already impoverished and disempowered many of its members.

These institutions tend to have had an historical presence and carry considerable weight because of it. The most significant of these institutions is patriarchy operationalised through the family foremost. Consistently women are held inferior to men across different patriarchal societies. Other social institutions are those regarding caste and ethnicity. Most of these relations have been encoded economically over time through labour practices, that are for most part exploitative. The other important institutions are those of religion – particularly the caste system and ethnic and minority groupings. Labour interactions are the fourth major group in particular – child labour, bonded labour and informal sector workers.[1]

Contractual (Equal) Institutions

These institutions are premised on "objective" truths and values existing independent of their members. They place importance on performance and management and tend to be task oriented, with instrumental relations with their members. They seek uniformity and homogenise individual experiences and differences according to "objective" truths and values so as to measure, consolidate and distribute the resources within. The institution makes no difference between knowledge and information and sees both as bits of commodities to be owned, bought and sold to the person who can pay the most money, without value underpinnings. These institutions presume a 'level playing field' that allows their members to own the institution equally based on their inclination to do so; in reality, these institutions exacerbate existing inequities and allow the accumulation of homogenised resources by powerholders within traditional exploitative institutions. They support individual and collective expression, creativity and agency only as far as its increases efficiency of their performance.

The members of these institutions feel isolated and are forced to look to their own survival even if such action in inimical to themselves in the future and to others in the present. . The emphasis on individualism places the burden on structural inequities on the individual, resulting in "blaming the victim." These institutions focus on their members as numbers and aim to distribute their resources equally and protect the rights of their members, with no special consideration of past / historical inequities. The systems of distribution and protection are often biased and insensitive to the needs of all, since they tend to be created by those who have historically been powerful. The institutional reflections focus on task delivery and are limited to their own maintenance and ongoing survival in current situations. This kind of reflection also ensures that the biases towards the powerful remain hidden behind the 'objectivity' of their values and the compulsions of the immediate.

These institutions are relatively new phenomena. Most of the modern institutions fall into this category – including the modern states and the corporate market institutions. Though these institutions have become more powerful only in the last two hundred or so years – with the use of modern, western science – they have rapidly consumed and eradicated many of the globe's non-renewable natural resources. They have created unprecedented, unaccounted accumulation of capital in the last few decades and have served to isolate and alienate many of its members by commodifying and trading on all human experience to an unprecedented degree.

The two major institutions include the state and capitalist structures including credit groups who have now come to span the globe.

Affirmative (Equitable) Institutions

These institutions are premised on affirmative values. They place importance on individuals and their experiences and as well as the relations that they form with their members. They consider differences as being crucial for transformation and seek to engage with differences positively. They do not hierarchialise their members respecting each of them for the different contributions they make. They consider it necessary for information and knowledge to be freely available and circulated and seek to reflect on and add value to information collected with an open consideration of the ethics involved. They recognise the importance of the metis of the members and place significance on this form of knowing. They actively foster individual and collective self-expression, creativity and agency. They aim to distribute resources equitably taking into consideration historical inequities as well as individual differences. They protect the rights of all their members paying special attention to the vulnerabilities caused by past inequities. They are owned by their members and exist as support mechanisms for the better functioning of individual and collective interests. Their survival is dependent on the will of all their members. The institution is part of the creative lives of its members and provides the infrastructure for its members to fulfill their creative potential. They are willing to be self-reflective and they transform into new forms depending on the needs of their members. Their reflection includes both their past actions as well as the consequences to the future. Such affirmative institutions are often very young; they often co-exist within other exploitative and liberal institutions and are still riddled with contradictions that exist in the larger world.

These institutions are rare in worlds of experience of poor people

Agency

Agency is the ability of the individual to create and maintain relations of her own volition, to determine the value of the resources she accesses and controls in transactions within these relations, and to be able to access resources that is essential for her self-expression and creativity when she wishes to. It is the extent to which she is able to create, own and transform institutions that she belongs to and is able to seek justice for violations of her freedoms and person.

It is possible to conceive of three kinds of agencies.

Compelled/forced

The agency of the individual is overridden by priorities of the institution she belongs or is forced to belong to. The individual cannot own and transform the institution and is forced to act within the institutional framework even when such rules are inherently discriminatory and inimical for survival and growth. She is not allowed any expression and therefore cannot be creative. Her institutional membership is contingent on her utility value and is terminated once her utility is considered over. Her access to resources is mediated by the discriminatory practices of the institution and there is often no recourse to justice. Failure to conform to the institution's rules result in exclusion, punishment and death. Individulas caught in situations qualified here evolve a host of coping strategies that are inwardly directed. (See the chapter 6 further elaboration on this)

<u>Surviving</u>

The individual acts within the boundaries of the institution to ensure her individual survival and well-being. Her self expression and creativity has to exist within role defined boundaries of the institution, and she can enjoy the benefits of the institution as long as she is able to conform to its boundaries. She is allowed transform the system only so far as to increase its functioning and cannot influence its values and rules. She can access resources and justice systems only if she belongs to and stays within the institutional boundaries. Failure to do so results in loss of power and resources. Therefore the stragies invented by the individuals trapped in circumstances of elaborated here are survival strategies that are other- directed (See the chapter 6 further elaboration on this)

Creative

The individual has a sense of personal and shared ownership and responsibility about the institution and its resources. She is able to express herself freely and this expression allow personal and systemic tranformation. She is able to create, modify and monitor existing institutional values and rules for her personal and the collective well-being; She is freely able to use the resources of the system as long as it does not impinge on the interests of others in the present and in the future. She is able to regulate her own expressions and uses the system to support her individual and collective reflection. Individuals inhabiting conditions highlighted here evolve transformative strategies that are inner-directed. (See the chapter 6 further elaboration on this)

Conclusion

In the following pages the way the life circumstances of the poor are produced as a result of the interplay of the three axes namely, agency, instituitions and the intreactions between the two constitute impoverishing prcesses will be described analytically.

To gound the understaning of the following chapters, select life histories from each of the five countries will be presented for perusal for those who wish to move from stories to analysis of the stories. However this does not detain those readers who desire to return to the stories after reading the analysis.

The chapter following the compendium of stories is on the institutional contexts of impoverishment. This elaborates on the two crucial types of institutions that contain predominantly impovershing tendencies for the poor, namley traditional and modern instituions. Gathering insights from the stories themselves this chapter enumerates various types of interactions that these institutional contexts generate and their impoverishing consequences for the poor. The chapter does not discuss the affirmative institutions at any length for they are rare, hardly evidenced in the stories and, even if existing, yet to be accessible to the poor.

Chapter 6 is about the larger socio-cultural- economic- political processes that impinge on the lives of the poor predominantly keeping them poor, when not rendering them poorer. In keeping with the understanding of poverty elaborated in the current chapter on framework, this chapter focusses its attention on the only dominant mode by which people living in poverty are forced to live in poverty viz, by being reduced to mere working bodies. Here poverty is argued as a comprehensive experience of having to live as working bodies as well as the attendant disabilities acruing on account of that body-dependent existence. This is explained as a relational outcome of the interaction between human agency and institutional forces.

The Chapter 7 on agency aspires to give a fair account of the various strategies evolved by the poor against all odds to recuperate their humaness. Instead of taking on a romanticising or celebratory stance vis-à-vis the poor people's agency-exerciseing strategies, this chapter approaches the myriad of stagies by which poor make sense of their personal universes with sensitivity and caution. Thus there is an attempt made to classify the modes of exercising agency into three types. They are: inward-directed agency, other-directed agency and inner-directed agency. The chapter ends with the plea as to which mode of exercising agency all those who are commited to development of the poor should stand by and show solidarity with.

The report concludes with a chapter on the possible ways out of the poverty traps. Principally written on a suggestive mode rather than on the prescriptive mode, this chapter argues for reinstatement of responsibilty-structure in various institutional forces starting from family to global insitutions. Also suggested is the return of the 'political' in spheres that have become apolitical in the last decades.

References

Baulch, B and McCulloch, N. 1998. Being poor and becoming poor: Poverty stauts and poverty transition in rural poor. *IDS Working Paper* No 79. Brighton, IDS

Editrial. 2000. Marginalisation of Tribals. *Economic and Political Weekly*; November 18.

Giddens, Anthony (1984) *The Constitution of Society. Introduction of the Theory of Structuration*. Berkeley. University of California Press

Kabeer, Naila, and Ramya Subrahmanian. 1996. *Institutions, Relations and Outcomes: Framework and Tools for Gender-aware Planning*. University of Sussex, U.K.: Institute of Development Studies.

Keith Hart. 1999. *The Memory Bank: Money in an Unequal World*,

Michael & Nunn, P . 1994. *Paradox and Healing: Medicine, Mythology & Transformation*; Greenwood,; Paradox Publishing

Narayan, D, Chambers, R, Shah, M K, Petecsch, P. 2000b. *Voices of the Poor/; Crying out for Change*, Newyork . OUP

Narayan,D with Patel,R, Schafft,K, Rademacher,A and Koch-Schulte,S. 2000a.*Voices of the ooor: Can any one hear us?*. Newyork, OUP

World Development Report. 2000/2001. *Removing Social Barriers and Building Social Institutions, Washington*

VII

Popular Strategies or Unpopular? Working With Poor and Marginalized in Their Own Terms

The conspiracy of various impoverishing forces impacting on the lives of the poor has reduced the poor to their mere *labouring bodies*. The intensity of such reduction has been progressively accelerated in the past decade, as families and individuals slipping into poverty happens much faster than their counterparts in previous generation. With the arrival of modernity, the institutionalization of the standards and frameworks of the non-poor has only added more momentum to such reduction. Simultaneous to the processes that reduced poor to *labouring bodies* and to body-dependent existence, is the unleashing of another tendency of these processes that deprives the poor of their personhood and reduce them to *non-persons*. The latter is equally debilitating, and in poor persons' lives more devastating.

For the poor, the moments at which they resorted to and lived doing mind-dependent work were the most creative moments, at which they felt that they had exercised their agency. But life in poverty did not permit such moments that yield economic gain. Since the roles that poor occupy in various capacities as factory workers, brick kiln labourers, agricultural coolies, rickshaw pullers, sex workers etc. are replaceable by another self-same person, the poor find their identity getting flattened to the one-dimensionality that they wish to get out all their lives – the identity as *labouring bodies*. For the wider society the poor is interchangeable with another poor – be it in domestic work or sexwork. The impossibility to inscribe their individual signatures into the type of work they do, the inability to get positively and economically valued for the same and, even more tragically, the incapability to afford time and space to insinuate their unique presence seem to have more catastrophic consequences than their starvation. As rickshaw pullers, domestic servants, porters, beggars, they do not have a presence in the landscape and mindscape of the society at large. Who remembers the face of the last porter or the rickshaw puller one hired? For the non-poor they have only utility value. They are as good only as the functions they perform. And they are mere extensions of the tools they use – the trolleys, rickshaws etc.

To be reduced to the capacity of *non-person* is to be deprived of the control over time, space and metis in ones' life. An important aspect of loss of control is the gross devaluation of one's time, space and metis. Indeed, in poor persons' lifehistories there are only instances of how poor have been forced to lose control over time, space and metis. Poor persons' time is not their resource, their space is alienable and metis is discreditable. They cannot even afford to have a storied life, which is nothing but an appropriation of the social time, space and wisdom into personally significant time, space and metis in one's life.

But these cannot become the last words on the poor and their poverty. The poor do not want to be *non-persons*, as any dignified person does not want to be. Poor continue to resist and do not take as their essence the flattening of their selves into one-dimensional existence, namely *labouring bodies*. They evolve their resistance and defiance to it in myriad ways, some of them are imaginative and creative and many of them are reactive and retreative. Their agency is in constant engagement with the structures they have been confronted with, in all times and spaces despite their existence under impoverishing conditions. They have always sought to achieve a well-rounded personhood for themselves. They have always engaged in evolving strategies and inventing newer ways to imaginatively achieve their personhood. They deeply detest being reduced to *labouring bodies* and subsequently to *non-persons*. They have always demonstrated this urge in ways that would be defined by the mainstream society as crude, senseless and violent. They have been making their claims to personhood very loudly and clearly. It is just that the mainstream society would characterize it as cacophony. They have been constructing their personally significant personhood in utter silence and solitude. The acknowledgement that they have been reduced to the status of *non-person* and, even worse still, that they themselves are *non-persons* in their own personal understanding, comes to great relief in their hesitation to narrate their lifehistories[i].

Though the poor seem to be engaged in their efforts for survival all the time, it is more apparent than true. For all practical purposes they seem to work towards renewing their body's strength for continual exertion for survival, but this is always accompanied by a carefully felt desire to seek meaning for their lives by defining their location in the larger universe. If, in their struggle for survival, large number of poor has not taken to criminal, immoral and violent means, it is because of their desire to seek existential significance even in whatever small acts they do morally. In the context of the cautiously invented ethical frameworks that give intense personal meaning, they are acutely conscious of their connectedness with the fellow humanity as well as with whatever divine forces they invent to govern their destiny. They want to make sense not only to themselves but also to the fellow humanity whose constituents may be real or imagined, living or dead, proximate or distant, and known or unknown. They want each one of their individual acts to be validated by them, beneficial to them and able to strengthen their morale. On the contrary their connection with the fellow humanity is also deeply renewed through the acts of teaching a lesson to the ones who betrayed and belittled them, conveying strong message to the ones who bothered them and settling scores with the ones who caused troubles to them.

Thus, the poor persons' lives are not spent in mere renewal of body alone but also of their connectedness to their consciously chosen fellow humanity. That is why in poor persons' narration of their lifehistories they make continuous references to other significant (for good or bad reasons) persons; they come off as being connected to their fellow humanity in all moments of their existence; and they continuously involve themselves in communication, silent or overt, with others. In their silent acts of refusal to take any violent means of survival, is hidden their loud celebration of the connectedness to whatever larger universe they create and fill with significant persons – real or imagined. In their loud celebration of their connectedness one also could see their transcendence to *persons* from *non-persons*, in whatever personally significant ways.

Faced with a wide range of forces that deprive them of their personhood and rupture their sense of connectedness by forcing them to become *laboring bodies*, the poor have evolved many strategies for regaining and retaining their personhood. These are besides the host of strategies they have invented for mere survival of their working bodies, as we have elaborated in the previous chapter. The dignity of the poor is the function of their successful retention of their personhood.

Yet, while all the strategies they evolve are of immense personal significance to them, not all of them alter the conditions within which they have to retain and regain their personhood. In fact, many such strategies that the poor evolve are actually significant to personal life of poor as they generate intense meaning for them, but tragically they do not critically engage with the institutional and structural arrangements within which they have been forced to struggle for retention of their personhood. In other words, the invention of strategies by the poor for acquiring their personhood does not make life better for their next generation, not even for their next day. Instead of critically engaging with the structures that deny them personhood and reorganizing them in ways that would ensure freedom to persons with no efforts (as it would be the natural outcome of the new structures one can create and recreate), the poor are mostly engaged in strategies that have least significance structural transformation, albeit their enormous personal significance.

Typologies of agency

The responses of the poor to the impoverishing conditions have been varied. Despite the flattening effects produced by the impoverishing forces, the poor have been evolving strategies and adding a sense of aliveness to their living. The various types of responses and strategies that poor evolve to engage with the structures around them and institutional contexts, in which these occur, as well the directions into which their agencies are moved can be diagrammatically represented as follows:

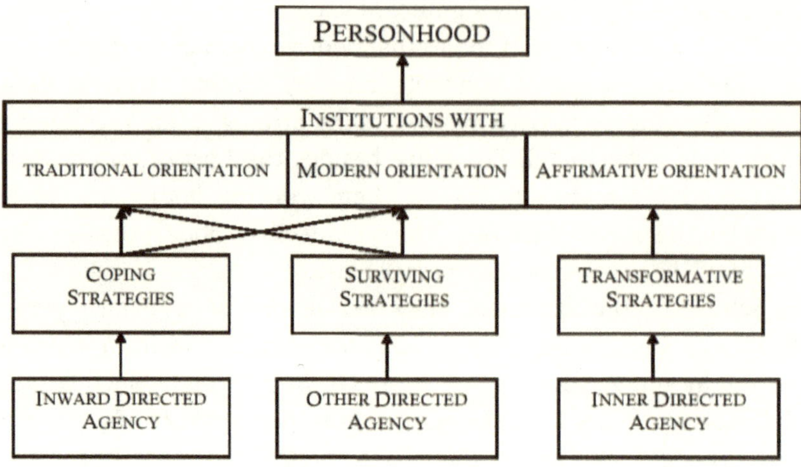

Figure 2: The Agency Dynamic

Inward-directed agency

The various strategies adopted by the poor are acutely inward-directed, for the harshness of the outer world would immediately punish them for externalizing them in the real world. It is inwardly-directed

1. In the sense of their operational terrain being limited only to boundaries of the acts and situation within which the poor operate.
2. In that these strategies are highly personal acts that do not seek the approval and consensus from the outer world, thus removing possibilities of collective action.
3. In one more sense viz., the burden of finding meaning for all these strategies rests only on the individual actor who adopts these strategies and not derivative of the organic external relationship.

All these somehow ensure that they are discrete, fragmented and inconsistent. They do not alter the boundaries in the real world, but create boundaries and division in the inner world of the poor to give themselves a sense of aliveness and forward movement. The various strategies adopted under this type of agency can be characterized as **coping strategies**. They have three types of responses namely fatalist, retreatist and metaphoristic.

Coping strategies

Faced with continual denial of their unique personhood and confronted by structures that take monstrous dimensions in the perception of poor, there are vengeful attempts by the poor to construct meanings for themselves in way that makes significant sense to them. There is a variety of ways by which they cope with the experiences of denial of their individual selfhood and reduction to the status of non-persons. Most of these strategies give them tremendous sense of self-importance and help them to see themselves as significant actors in control of their own destiny. They provide joyfulness and instant psychological security, however transitory and false they may be. They locate them at the central point of the smaller inter-personal universe they create. Their deeds are redefined as heroic in the context of small acts they do. They give them a sense of control over time, space and metis. In sum the strength to see the next day in life is renewed both bodily and *person*ally.

These strategies express in different type of responses by which they have constructed collectivities that may not be positively regarded by the wider societies, yet personally very significant to them. They are as follows- they have resorted to fatalism; they have taken up flight from reality; they have engaged in structuring of their everyday survival processes in ways that give them a sense of progress and forward movement; they have adhered to belief systems that allay their suffering today and promises a better tomorrow; they have inverted the agreed categories, forms and categories; and they have added an element of heroism even for the socially undervalued work they do by rearranging the comparable standards of heroism. They do this by evolving conclaves of virtues within the boundaries of which the heroic spirit is extolled for adherence to the virtues. These localized conclaves of virtues do not make much sense outside their territories.

Fatalist

In the face of extreme loneliness and utter hopelessness generated by impoverishing forces, the poor's inventiveness works in the direction of creating conclaves of virtues and gamut of belief systems that are either derivative of the larger moral-religious universe they belong to, or of their deep personal experience. So the poor often seem to resort to localized belief systems that extol the virtues of the poor and promise awaiting justice in future. They also invent virtues that will give them deep personal significance, such as the belief "that if one helps another poor he will be rewarded with benefits in future". They come out with virtues of being kind and good to everyone and these despite their utter poverty give them a regular victory in the struggles for even mere physical survival. Their not resorting to immoral means even in the context of starvation and pennilessness, give them deep satisfaction. They often talk about their acts of kindness and help rendered to known and unknown, as giving enormous amount of self-importance to themselves. There is also tremendous amount of joy in defining their personal goodness around their kindness and personal care shown to the near and dear ones. The profound satisfaction they derive in demonstration of love, care and attention to the children, elders, men and women, both inside the family and outside it, is also accompanied by the belief in the oncoming of rewards in manifolds. All these strategies are attempts at making suffering bearable and at piecing together the fragmentation of their selves.

Through this inward-directed agency, the poor are able to establish control over their time but only in their personal world that may not have much significance for the real world. In the personal world they inhabit, time is compartmentalized into suffering time and rewarding time. The former is seen as so extended even to cover the entire life span and the latter may arrive any time. The unpredictability of these two is what makes life bearable today. The suffering may end any moment or may not end at all, and so may rewards. So, that is what carries the individual poor into next day, as well-rounded and unfragmented persons.

The fatalistic response and strategies could also happen in solidarity with others who share their vision of the world as determined by interconnected events, thus persuading the poor to see logical connection between their present existence and past - which explains as to why they have slipped into poverty in a manner that makes poverty bearable today, as much as the connection between present and future, where the poverty may have an end.

Retreatist

The tragic outcome of life in poverty is the very impossibility of seeing the logical outcome of one's course of life. If one were to make such an analysis and predict the actual course that life would take in this given birth, one may not be able to answer the calls of dreams, which know no logic and dominate the living styles of poor and non-poor. But in the case of poor the soul-corroding awareness of logical connections between life events and what exactly they have in its reserves, will keep knocking the doors of the poor as they directly engage with very clearly limited possibilities. In the poor the awareness about the impossibilities in life is broader than that of the non-poor. The perfect knowledge of what is not possible in life has to be confronted in its nakedness in every moment of their engagement with real world. While fatalism may help to reconcile to this and expect the reward in unknown future, this may not be everybody's option. It is that section among poor, who, with the sound knowledge of impossibilities in life, are still unable to take refuge in fatalism. It is they who retreat from this very reality and retire in a world created by themselves through altering of mind states or participation in fantasy world. In these personal worlds they are secure, larger-than-real and central.

Metaphoristic

Metaphorisation is defined as the outcome of the efforts by which ordinary is turned into extraordinary through the processes of inversion, reversal, hierarchisation, instinctification, mimicking, objectisation and episodification. The process by which the metaphorisation of life happens in the lives of the poor is one such coping strategy. The harsh demands on the lives of the poor for survival call for an existence in continual exertion of body. This forces them to engage in activities that tend to stupefy their sensibilities. One of the reasons why poor call themselves poor is because of their inability to create events in their lives. Filled with incidents of ensuring survival, poor find it difficult to make life eventful. This manifests itself in the form of indivisibility of their time in ways that make personal sense to the poor and add personal significance to them.

In this kind of response which is inward-directed the individuals would engage in structuring of their time in very imaginative ways. These strategies would make tremendous personal sense, but only under the conditions brought about by impoverishing process, yet would not make much economic sense, nor would it engage with the impoverishing forces critically. The time would be divided into significant episodes only in the deep personal memories whose appropriateness and significance need not necessarily have wider consensus. Thus these will be very lonely, secluded individualized personal acts that do not have structural significance, or they are performed and validated in the company of selected members of the collectivity who subscribe to the significance of these personal acts.

They are trying to create a sense of meaningfulness to their lives by constructing personally significant universes and sensible cosmologies. They have circumscribed for themselves relevant structures involving limited spaces, scarce time and the network of significant people available to them. Also, the attribution of heroic spirit to their otherwise stressful and battle-ridden existence is still a hallmark of poor people's efforts to rise above the body-dependent living.

The various manners by which the poor make their existence very meaningful and bearable to them are through the process of metaphorisation of the otherwise dull, drab and drudgery-ridden existence. In their everyday work for survival there is so much that incapacitates the poor from exercising their agency. Not only this, but it also denies and erodes the significance that can accrue to their lives. This happens by pushing the poor to depend on their body dependent existence and deny their control over time and space. The poor thus have to personalize the time and space only from the opportunities available through the cracks of the social mosaic. These processes of personalisation are least significant in terms of the structural changes that they may effect. But they may be personally very significant for the poor. Each one need elaboration and exposition.

Inversion and Reversal: Inversion is a process by which the established order, meaning and practices are inverted so as to produce opposite or contrary effects. Reversal is the attempt to take up the positions not meant for the persons concerned. One such strategy is to invert the social universe that the people occupy. Though on numerous occasions the society itself has created many such liminal spaces in which the rebellion of the marginalised could find expression and full play, even this marginal space is not available to many poor. One may here recall that even during those occasions in which the rest of the society is venting out its repressed rebellion in the form of holy celebration and other ritualised occasions, one would still find many marginalised members of the society still playing roles they have always performed. These hapless masses have been forced to find spaces elsewhere to exhibit their rebellion. Worse still, the rebellion of the poor is stigmatised and treated as an unwarranted response. Thus, having been compelled to retire in the crevices of the society, the poor still invent strategies that engage only within the boundaries of the limited spaces of the crevices. Therefore, they invert the meanings of the mainstream world, reverse the categories of the wider society, mimic the practices and styles of the mainstream world. We often find evidences of the inversion and reversal of social role and social structures in the form of the sexworker trying to use socially accepted categories such as "fieldwork" or "going on line" or "entertainment business" or "going for dance". The scavenger women would call it "municipality work". The street boy would call it a "choice". The beggars would call their work "Money catching" or "earning". They use these categories as a response against the stigma and degradation which society puts them into. They convert the very processes of being reduced to poverty and to body-dependent existence into meaningful experiences and even turn them into defenses. Not only are these expressed in terms of merely changing names but in terms of practices too. We have instances in which the scavenger women maintain an impeccable and spotless house as well as personal cleanliness that is striking and a strong statement against the unclean work she does otherwise. Similarly, many of the sexworkers often aspires to create a well-ordered household as well as a family as a response to the disorderly life that they themselves acknowledge to lead. They strive very hard to give semblance of order and organization to the family by bringing social fathers even at the cost of their personal happiness, or even if it means paying for the maintenance of the social father who often turn out to be lazy, nuisance-creators and spendthrifts. The same goes true of the beggar and homeless who establishes a home and a neatly circumscribed house even in pavements and other open spaces. We could often see them demarcating the spaces in the platforms into kitchen, sleeping rooms and doorsteps, apart from maintaining it so religiously by sprinkling water in the so-called front yard of the imagined house and keeping the place so clean and tidy. Even more curiously they used to refer to these places using the names we normally reserve for a full-fledged house/homes.

The other form of making work bearable is **"deliberate misunderstanding"** which is used very effectively against the drudgery and the drabness of the work and life itself. The **"deliberate misunderstanding"** happens in the form of taking begging and street life as an "educational experience" or "as a learning experience". The **"deliberate misunderstanding"** also manifests itself in taking the socially stigmatized work they do as an excuse for some purposeful social activity such as involvement in drug peddling as a cover for looking for a lost daughter. Or a young girl becoming a bride in the family where the groom is an old man, yet she takes immense amount of satisfaction in the fact that she could get good food, something she cannot hope to get in her family of birth. Or taking the work as a teashop owner as offering more satisfaction and self-control rather than work in a government office. Or treating the rickshaw pulling work as more freedom ensuring than the work under a fodder shop owner. There are many poor who invent very many meaningful ways of being poor.

Objectisation: They are very inclined to turning themselves into objects if that is going to give them deep satisfaction and sense of purpose. We see young girls volunteering themselves to become objects of exchange only because it redeems the family they belong to from the chronic poverty. This happens more in the case of women, and with globalisation even men are not spared. There are instances of sexworkers who agree to becoming sellers of their bodies under extremely distressing circumstances. They suddenly realise their agency in being able to make financial contribution. This happens in the context of the men refusing to be responsible enough to take care of the family. Pitted against a gross failure of the larger structures such as the State and community, the self-willed objectification becomes a tragic triumph and ironical celebration of agency of the women. This process of self-determined objectification does not leave men out either. More and more number of men has been forced to realise their agency only in the terrain of their body dependent existence. Even their limited body dependent success is celebrated as a major triumph and significant contribution.

Instinctification: This is not unconnected to process of objectisation of the persons. In the lives of many poor, there have been attempts to suspend their consciousness and replace that with instincts. In fact, it is not just replacement but a gradual conversion of the consciousness into instincts. Many Dalit men and women in their everyday interaction have to remember the boundaries that they cannot transgress as well as the behavioural responses they have to adopt in the presence of the non- Dalit members. Instead of keeping it in the consciousness and giving it a significance that they actually refuse to attach, they junk the awareness of the same into the complex of instincts thereby reducing them to the levels of body processes. Many sexworkers too mentioned about their refusal to self-willingly and self-consciously take part in the exact processes of permitting their bodies to be consumed by the clients, by becoming objects or only a bundle of instincts at time of their bodies being consumed by the clients. They talk about the fact that their clients very often complain about their non-cooperation and flaccidity, least realizing that it is their way of protest and rebellion. It is also their demonstration of non-participation in the experiences of reduction to non-persons. Another context in which the awareness and consciousness of their marginalisation and their forced participation in them are turned into instincts is in survival situation in the lives of poor. The very manner by which they instinctively extend their arms for alms and, their instinct for fleeing at the sight of the assessment of threats and troubles from the police and other bad elements etc are done by drawing from the complex of instincts, which are mostly solidified consciousness. Their very survival depends on the rejection of their own conscious participation in their personal degradation and marginalisation.

Hierarchisation: The hierarchisation of the ordinary experience is one more strategy to give them a sense of aliveness to their existence. The poor tend to construct their experiences into several episodes, each superior to the previous one. By dividing the experiences into many such episodes, they give themselves a sense of movement to their life graph and also act as incentives for the younger ones to aspire to reach the higher levels. Among the children in the streets there is well-defined organisation of residents into those with more experiences, so privileged with better places for sleeping in the nights. They also get better respect from others thereby forcing the young generation to aspire for the role as the head of the organisation. Even among the beggars we have such instances of who get better places to beg and who has the first right to divide the money when it is given in bulk to one beggar, and so on and so forth. This makes the new entrants to make their lives bearable as they have something to aspire for, namely position of importance among the beggars.

The hierarchisation of experiences manifests itself in many forms. Among the beggars it is their ability to elicit utmost sympathy from the charitable public as well as the ability to identify right kind of person who would give alms. Among the rickshaw pullers the senior most ones are those who could handle a variety of customers and classify them as well as negotiate with them for smarter hiring charges. The brilliant rickshaw puller is the one who attract more customers and get himself caught and harassed by the police the least. In the case of sexworkers, the most experienced and therefore deserving more respect is the one who have smart enough to wriggle her out of the police raid, the troubling customer and from the custody of vigilance homes. The novices are the ones who have either confronted a smaller number of situations of this kind or get caught even in those few encounters. Thus, for the individual in the respective situations the acquisition of smartness and the skills become the points at which they feel like moving up in the imaginary ladder. It gives them a tremendous sense of forward movement to them.

Episodification: The whole process of episodification is another important strategy used by the poor to make life bearable. Even though the poor have been compelled to live a highly routinised life that has been denied of the energy and resource to add variety due to the emergence of market forces which have increasingly colonized all spheres of human life including even the narrow interstices, the poor have been able to find their own spaces and bent of mind to give themselves a sense of variety by inscribing certain forms of cultural markers in the otherwise routinised course of life. Many of the domestic servants, beggars, street children, disabled and ragpickers would divide the work situations and the type of work they do in such a manner that it gives them a sense of eventfulness in life on the one hand as well as the feeling of crossing many episodes in a given day or week or even months, on the other hand. The beggars move from one place to another in a given day by marking each place with one type of significance and other with another -- One place for food, the other place for coins yet another place for dress and so on and so forth. The street boy or girl moves from one railway station to another in search of bathing places and sleeping places. The domestic servant divides the work in such a manner that one day is assigned for cleaning the halls in the houses where she works and another day for cleaning the toilets and bedrooms etc. The very keen participation in the cultural media such as film watching, TV watching in bus stands as well as in other public places, and other forms of entertainments is an attempt at marking the drab existence with cultural dividers that give them a sense of movement across zones in life.

Other-Directed Agency

The other-directed agency here refers to any situation in which the person realizes her agency only in relation to the structure whose normative order is conformed with and unchallenged. The consummation of agency is achieved only in compliance with disciplinary practices and procedures normalized by the structure. The structure may be traditional or modern. Here in the context of our present concern, we see the poor's willing assumption of non-poor virtues and adherence to the standards of the very same forces and institution that impoverish them. In other words, the poor adopt those strategies that would enable them to survive, even if it means subjecting themselves to the same disciplining procedures and practices of precisely of the same institutions and collectivities that impoverished them in the first instance. Here they adopt the moral frameworks, ethical standards and other scales of evaluation of human worth, more as a strategy than as a worldview. The desire for realizing the individual agency comes from within, though meanings for such acts arise from outside Thus they may undergo a training programme or migrate to a new place as demanded by the State so that they may become eligible for the rewards and resources, albeit their refusal to take part in them soulfully as a worldview. There may be other instances in which they may respond positively and willingly to the very manner of construction of the 'good' servant, 'good' daughter, 'good' daughter-in-law etc. so as to qualify themselves for the social rewards and economic resources. In all these cases there is a willingness to be co-opted by the very same systems and institutions that impoverish them in absolute terms. Thus, if the poor can ever have their presence established and significantly noticed, it would be only when they fit into the frameworks held up as appropriate by the non-poor.

It must be remembered that the virtues of the poorer are hardly self-determined, even when they find their votaries in the non-poor segment. They are defined for and circulated among the poor by the non-poor only because it serves the latter's collective goals and vested interests. Not only these non-poor as individuals construct the contours and contents of the virtues for the poor so as to give them the concession of acceptance and space in the exclusive territories of the non-poor as well as of the institutions they dominate and control -- the most important among them being the State and the whole lot of its arms, like educational institutions, hospitals, banks, courts etc.

When deploying this set of strategies there will be willingness also to deny the significance of their own traditional and habitual ways of restructuring time, and adhere to the compartmentalization of time as induced by the dominating institutions. Spatially they would adopt the standards of measurement followed by the dominant institutions and their members as well as the eligibility conditions specified for the same. Thus, they may resort to exclusions on their own. Under these circumstances, the knowledge system of the past and ancestors will be actively discredited by the poor themselves and celebration of even the negligible acquisition of wisdom subscribed to by the dominant section of the society will characterize the strategies adopted here. Here the individuals would become agents of the dominant worldview that may be Brahminical at one end and modernist at the other end of the spectrum in India and Nepal, and Islamic in Bangladesh and Pakistan and ethnic and communist/modernist in Vietnam. During the last decade the globalizing world has made the so-called virtues of globalization (which are basically the virtues of the dominant sections even among the non-poor) the common virtues of all and sundry into which even the non-poor have been initiated.

Standing unintelligible to a host of institutions and the non-poor members in them, the poor experience many incidents of denial, deprivation and invalidation. The only way to make any sense in these situations is to take on the language, standards and pattern of the system. But we have seen in the previous chapter as to how poor could not afford to become acceptable to these institutions even when they ultimately resort to doing so, because of their inability to invest time, and resources to acquire the capacities. Adopting the institutional pathways legitimized by the institutions is costly due to the hidden costs, let alone the visible ones. They cannot go back to adhering to the ways of their traditional and primordial collectivities, for they have already been delegitimised and discredited by the modern institutions. So, the possibility of moving out of non-personhood to personhood is erased by the interlocking of these two processes.

Poor person's realization of his agency thus receives a serious blow. They have been forced to define their significance only against yardsticks legitimized by the institutions they have no control over. Therefore, they compel themselves to construct their sense of personhood in terms of the cultural codes defined by the non-poor and their institutions. We have many instances of poor forcing themselves and being forced to measure up to the expectation of the systems that have control over the resources crucial for the survival of the poor. They adopt these strategies for survival. The public sphere, in which the poor operate for mere survival, is ridden with tendencies that reduce poor persons to adopt strategies in ways that seem to render them incapable of realizing their essence. The spots in the memoryscape of the non-poor-dominated society are available only for these poor who act good, behave well and conduct themselves appreciably in the perceptions of the non-poor and the institutions they steer. It is a good household servant who does not steal money; it is an honest rickshaw puller who returns the purse the customer has forgettingly left behind, it is a porter who returns the extra rupee note that the client has inadvertently given away, who are declared virtuous and remembered. The uniqueness of the individual poor is the concession of the non-poor. The graduation from non-person to person is possible only if it is movement is along the tracks already laid by the non-poor.

But when the poor ultimately choose to adopt the standards of the mainstream world, and subject themselves to its disciplinary regimes, it is a choice they make on their own after considering the merits of doing so, however other-directed these choices and however misperceived their positive outcomes they may be. For example, when a woman agrees to be a good prisoner it is to ensure that her daughter survives against the odds that will be staked against her if behaves as a rude and problematic inmate. When many of the poor attend the work shop and training programmes on livestock breeding, sewing etc. it is out of their desire to make survival possible and also out of the hope to see whether doing so would help them realize their agencies in ways defined by the wider society. When individuals ultimately realize that their personal self-worth can be collected only in complicit participation in the institutional arrangements, it may underscore the triumph of

<u>Inner-Directed Agency</u>

Inner-directed agency is the product of inner realization about one's unfreedom and lack of control over one's time, space and metis. This realization is also accompanied by the inner desire and urge for alternative conditions of freedom. So inner-directed agency creates and deploys a set of strategies is aimed at transformation. Here the poor engage with the system critically and aspires to transform it through collective action. At the individual level they may work to undercut the hegemony of the system through the creative damaging they could cause to it by their acts of commission and omission. The end products of these strategies are many: One, establishment of control over their time and the right to structure, distribute and translate it in ways that would benefit them cumulatively; Second the reclamation of lost spaces and the freedom to access all other available social spaces for productive purposes; and thirdly and finally, the recuperation of credibility and economic significance for their wisdom, both inherited and acquired through experiences.

As regards transformative agency there are few instances recorded in the stories we have collected. The instances so mentioned often talk about the transformation at the personal level. Instances of structural transformation are rare. We have a situation in which the Dalits in a village have come together to fight against their oppression by the upper castes. They have managed to change the nature of relationship between the Dalits and non-Dalits, but are not sure of sustaining it. However even if these instances of transformation both at the level of individual selves and at the level of structure, the solidarity shown by the NGOs and individual actors of the State has been eminently enabling. But this itself is very rare and sporadic. The role of the State has been rarely that of transformation as it has largely exacted conformity to its own standards and disciplinary regimes. It might have enabled many families to transform themselves but only because they subjected themselves to the rigorous disciplinary processes of the State. We have however many instances in which the NGOs have shown tremendous unconditional support to build the morale of the poor. This may not have caused many consequences in the lives of the poor in terms of transformation in their life circumstances, yet it gave them a sense of control over their lives and hope for a better tomorrow. If there are few instances of eruption of the poor into spontaneous movements independent of any of these external agencies such as the State and NGOs it is the outcome of two interrelated tendencies: One, the absence of recognition and the presence of suspicion) of such independent and spontaneous collective organization by the poor as legitimate enough to deserve the support or solidarity of these organizations: The second, the arrival of market forces that severely distrust and deliberately destabilize any kind of solidarity between people leave alone the poor among them. As the market forces and the various services, they offer for profit are thrive only in the absence of parallel services being available free of cost or at an affordable price either from the traditional and communitarian institutions or the same services being derivative of strong ties between one member and the other as well as with the larger structures. Particularly the modern corporate services aspire to conspire with any agency that would make a hole in the social net that acts as the cushion against shocks and jolts. These holes then can be filled in by the commodified services and goods manufactured by these corporate forces. Thus, we see progressive growth of mistrust and suspicion in human relationship both at the interpersonal levels and between humans and their environments. The increasing suspicion for the credibility of neighbours, the quality of water, air, the quality of traditional health care is very much a recent phenomenon and the profit earned by the corporate houses by capitalizing on these fear, suspicion and anxiety cannot be overstated.

Taking Sides

Once these various types of agencies are classified, one has to decide about taking sides with them. The three types of responses of agencies of the poor namely, coping, surviving and transforming can happen under any one of the three institutional orientations, viz., traditional, liberal and affirmative, though ideally in the last of the three institutional orientations namely, affirmative institution one would see more of transforming agency. As explained in the previous chapter, the possibilities for realizing the transformative agency could have existed in institutions with traditional and liberal orientation, but due to interplay of several factors (some of which are intrinsic to the institutions themselves) they have lost their affirmative character, thereby eliminating chances for exercising transformative agency of the vast sections of its members. While many institutions with traditional orientation, such as family, caste, community, ethnic groups etc. have been drained of their affirmative orientation, the very logic inherent in institutions with modern orientations has cancelled out their affirmative character. This has created a set of conditions in which even the resourceful population has been forced to adopt coping and surviving modes of exercising agency. The poor thus have been compelled by the conspiracy of these forces to adopt coping modes of exercising agency mostly. Definitely there may be numerous instances in which poor would have exercised transformative agency, but by doing so they would have excluded themselves from the very universe from which the stories of the poor have been collected. But such optimism is not warranted, as even by quantitative standards of measurement the absolute number of poor is increasing rather than decreasing in the countries represented by the stories here.

The poor have been largely responsive to any efforts by any institution or organization to stand by their coping strategies. It is just they do not transform their lives in way that are significant and fulfilling to them. While the strength of the traditional collectivities such as family, and community to even stand by and validate their coping strategies has been continually eroded, the institutions with largely modern orientation such as the State, market and even development sector have absolutely refused to standby or validate the coping strategies of the poor. Even when they seem to welcome and validate surviving strategies of the poor, they hardly stand by them consistently. The tragedy is that even the development agencies such as NGOs and INGOs have at best stood by their coping strategies after eliminating the fatalist and retreatist ones, but have not moved significantly into validating and standing by their surviving strategies in practice, though in principle they express their desire and approval for them. But when it comes to standing by the transforming strategies their contribution is insignificant. However, what is deeply significant about the development sector is the realization that the creation of institutions with affirmative orientation rests as much as on taking unequivocal sides with the transforming strategies of the poor, as on their willingness to see themselves or correct themselves as one such institution in the first place. Perhaps because the institutions with modern orientations are least prepared to adopt affirmative values, they render themselves suspicious, when it comes to causing transformation in the lives of poor. The State has to become a responsible and responsive force to even comprehensively able to stand by the surviving strategies of the poor.

Notes and References

[1]A significant irony characterizing the lifehistory collection process is very reluctance on the part of the poor to see their lives as storied lives. All normal persons lead storied lives by which life can be segmented into a beginning followed by a high point and ending with a climax. It is because we see life as a story that we live our lives and wish to see a climax to it in a way that gives a sense of completeness to us. It is because life is seen as a story filled with interconnected events leading to a climax that it gives deep existential significance and so life is carried on. We all lead storied lives. And we want to tell these stories to others, for we see a message running through it. There is a proud announcement of acquisition of meaning and successful achievement of individual uniqueness and singular personhood in our narrating our lives as stories. In the life stories is subsumed the claim for a life lived uniquely and exclusively in a manner not matched by the rest or only matched by the best.

But the lives of poor and the whole lot of incidents progressively impoverishing the poor give them least enthusiasm for narrating it into a meaningful story. Perhaps the tragedies of the past have eroded the courage to see it as meaningful whole. This is one reason why poor hardly enter into storying their lives with enthusiasm and keen interest. Thus, constructing the poors' past into stories with narrative coherence becomes a joint exercise in which the listener takes more effort to seeing a pattern than the narrator who treats life as a collection of discrete events -- one connected to another only because it pushed them deeply into poverty.

The fragility of courage to enter into the past life is the outcome of both the lack of time to enter into such luxurious exercises due to their constant engagement with survival, and also of the absence of events made and controlled by the self-will of the poor.

But the weak enthusiasm or total reluctance on the part of the many, whose stories we have collected, to see their lives as storied lives itself speaks of the impoverishment they have undergone. It highlights the fragmented personhood or even the incomplete evolution and consummation of personhood in them, all due to the circumstances they find themselves in. In more than several instances the persons interviewed have shifted the burden of extracting a story-with-a-climax out of their lives to the listeners themselves, or at best they did it only in the shadow of solidarity shown by the listeners.

But tragically the stories do not bring out the dignity of the poor abundantly. Perhaps because the selection and writing of the stories happened with a particular intention of how people are living in poverty. There seems to be more focus on the experiences of poverty, rather than on how the poor people live in dignity despite the adversities that poverty surrounds them with.

VIII
Capturing Impoverisation Processes

Humans are always in the process of 'becoming'. To define them in terms of what they are *now* is much the same as defining the stream as a handful of static, non- flowing water, at that time of scooping it into our hands. In the social universes that people occupy, this continuous process of 'becoming' is not, by necessity, in one singular direction, characterized by the prevailing wisdom as a forward moment, with all the positive connotations attached to it, namely, betterment, growth, improvement and development. People in society are multi-directionally 'becoming'.

Specifically from our point of view, individuals, occupying various points of intersections where several social forces meet and converge, are 'becoming' rich from 'being' poor, 'becoming' poor from 'being' economically better-off, 'becoming' poorer from 'being' poor and so on and so forth. In spite of the multi-linear directions in which the 'becoming' of humans occurs, there is a vast majority of people in the globe who move in only one direction, namely 'becoming' poorer from 'being' poor across generations, across years, months and even days. Parallel to this is the alarming tendency of a significant *minority* 'becoming' richer from being rich on an *everyday* basis. Yet the luxury or the trauma of being caught in the dynamics of 'becoming' has not touched another important *majority*, the one that is frozen in time and exempted from becoming, namely the poorest. The poorest are the large chunk of the masses which live in poverty, experiencing the crushing intensity of poverty in the same degree across all the three grammatical divisions of time, viz., past, present and future.

This chapter attempts to capture the various processes that both structure a particular way of 'becoming' of individuals in Asia – 'being' poor to 'becoming' poorer, and perpetuate a particular way of 'being', namely, the poorest, who are congealed in poverty forever and caught in some sort of a time warp, as it were. The processes elaborated as operating on the lives of the 'becoming' poor and the 'being' poor are not exhaustive, nor do they claim to any degree of representativeness.

The processes described below are derivative of the specific observations, thus *only* reflective of the specific situations that have occurred in the lives of the people storied in the form of Lifehistories. There are possibilities for several other dimensions and aspects of the processes themselves, which fall outside the purview of what the life histories of the selected people seem to reflect. To a large extent, the following pages limit themselves to describing only those processes somehow commonly impacting and influencing the lives of poor in all the countries from which the stories have been collected, namely Bangladesh, India Nepal, Pakistan and Vietnam.

A close perusal of the Lifehistories guided us to organise the analysis of the processes along the lines of importance and proximity that various social forces have in the lives of poor. Thus, this chapter moves from commenting on those dominant processes whose terrain is very proximate to the lives of the poor, to that of distant terrains whose impact and influence on the life-circumstances of the poor is as intense and as significant.

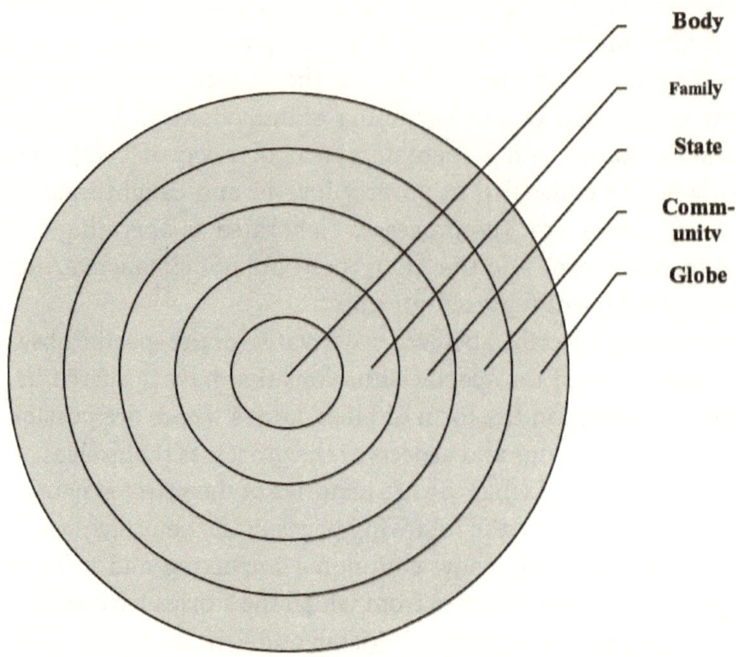

Figure 3: Concentric Circle of Impoverishment

In order of proximity, body, family, community (caste/tribal/religious), neighbourhood, nation and globe would occupy the sequenced spaces.

Each of the circles contains a force that determines the life circumstances of the poor. They unleash various processes that have the tendency to impoverish the people. Each process has gender and religious dimension qualifying it. When it comes to India and Nepal, caste dimension is also added to it.

These forces operate on people living in poverty either in unison or in combination with few others or in isolation from each other. They set in motion a series of impoverishing processes that cause poverty. These happen despite the all-out attempts constantly being made by the poor to organise their lives resolutely and imaginatively against the odds staked against them by these forces.

__Body as working machines__

What is astoundingly evident in the lives of poor is the continuous exertion of body, its mobility, agility and dynamism. Being very proximate to poor, yet not always under their control, body is the widely used force and acutely significant one at that. The stories of people in poverty are filled with imageries of their constantly moving from one place to another, their engagement in activity of one kind or other and their spending longer duration of wakeful hours in search of work and survival essentials like water and firewood etc. Unfortunately, in all these circumstances, it is the raw resources of the body that are in continual use. Indeed, it is these raw resources of the body of the poor that are singled out for trading by the economic forces, despite the poor persons' resistance to be reduced to mere body, despite their desire to move towards an existence in a creative unity between mind and body.

It is exactly because poor regard poverty as the condition in which there is a pressing compulsion to use *only* their body and its raw resources for survival, that the life out of poverty for them has come to mean the freedom to use the resources of mind in close and creative union with body for livelihood. Instead of privileging the 'thinking mind' as the only possible resource for living, the poor persons postulate a creative unity between the two and wish to live by the resources generated out of it. The fact that these are voiced by women perhaps renders justice to gender inequity and corrects the existing lacuna in the existing models of development, which tend to privilege mind over body and, by extension, devalue all that is the product of body -from its excreta to its re-productivity to its labour. The patriarchal design that undervalues women's contribution, both as producing *labourers* and reproducing the *labour* in them, thus, stands critiqued.

Consequently, we see two important processes that operate in the domain of body to result in poor becoming poorer. One is the brutal reduction of poor to a 'working body' and the second is the undervaluation of its contributions and resources. The outcomes of these two dominant processes are debilitating for the poor and they activate a reverse spiralling in which the only direction possible is movement towards the abyss of bottom.

The Conditions of Poverty

The conditions prevailing under the first process are many. The first condition of poverty is the necessity to use body as the sole resource for survival. Throughout the Lifehistories we find that the poor are being forced to define their self-worth in bodily terms. The whole processes of denial and deprivation, which we shall elaborate later under different sections, create the conditions for reducing the self-worth of the poor to the worth generated by body and its resources. Tragically the reduction begins at infancy itself. Such reduction, apart from rendering life dependent on the use of body and its resources, also disrupts the progressive appreciation of value accruing to humans as the wear and tear of the body in continual exertion undermine its exchange value when humans age. It is clear that only when freed from the compulsions of exchanging body and only when existence *is* the function of creative use of mind in wholesome union with body, there can be possibility for sustained investment in the progressive unfolding of capabilities in humans. That is why there is a premium placed by non-poor on continual investment in human growth and development, whereas poor invests only in the mere renewal of bodily energy to carry themselves to next day's work, only if available, that is.

If education and other capacity building and skill-building activities, and programme assume least significance in the lives of poor, it is because of the compulsions to make economic gains for the sheer survival from very early stage itself. Poor do not posses the economic wherewithal to afford 'deferred gratification' resulting from such investments made in education and other capacity building programmes. Thus, we have situations in poor people's lives in which even an infant is compelled to become an economically gainful worker. When we learn about a mother lending her newborn baby for a rent of Rs. 15/- per day to child beggars (who hopes to evoke quick sympathy from the public with a baby in their arms), we do not need a harsher testimony to this fact. Ironically, it is just the beginning.

If poor are becoming poorer, it is because they are coming under increasing compulsions, caused by forces at various levels, to rely upon their bodies and their raw resources for survival. These stories point to increasing compulsions that poor face to treat their body as the only asset, as only resource for survival. These compulsions impact the poor in various manners to set off processes of becoming poorer. Thus, two more conditions obtain:

1. The poor are forced to enter into economic transaction only with their body as primary capital. Here the body is not the carrier of marketable skills and capacities for the undervaluation of whatever residual skills that existed in it has preceded the points at which they enter economic transaction.

2. The body-dependent existence, into which people in poverty have been forced, further locks them into the limitations of time and space specific to the abilities of body. This entails a situation in which the temporal and spatial resources are used only for the purpose of renewal of body for the next day's labour and not for any further investment in skills and capacities that have market relevance.

The highly iniquitous and exploitative conditions in which the poor use body and its raw resource for economic gain, generates only as much benefits, in kind or in cash, as to renew the resourcefulness of the body for a very short duration of time, beyond which the body has to, perforce, engage in another round of economic transaction, for further renewal and survival. The fact that opportunities for continual gainful economic transaction are far fewer and fast drying up in the emerging circumstances only brings about undue hardship and distress upon the lives of the poor.

The Scenarios

Therefore, what we begin to see is the non-stop exodus of poor from their place of birth to strange and alien places in search of opportunities to transact with their bodies and their raw resources. The stories suggest that increasingly high percentage of poor is now living in places that are not their birthplaces. Contrastingly, even if they have the opportunity to live in places of their birth, their economically gainful work happens in other places. The constant mobility and the necessity to keep bodies in motion compel the poor to pay least attention to investment in skills and capacities.

The cost of self-renewal of the body for the next round of engagement with economic transaction, if ever it is available, is higher than that of the exact amount produced by the body in its first round of economic transaction. Thus, the demand for the involvement of other dependent members of the collectivity, be it family or kin-group, is intensified. This compels the poor to put to the optimal usage, not only her body but also that of the members of her collective - optimal usage not only in a given day but across all days in her life, since the best of the efforts still produce something less than what carries her to the next day.

This also spurs urgency, in response to which even children are turned into earning members. We have evidence to suggest as to how even the disabled members are evaluated on the scale of economic productivity and thus forced to engage in hard work. (We shall have occasion to elaborate on the conditions of disabled persons later). It is primarily because the very processes, that have subjected the previous generation to impoverishing conditions, are unleashed on the next generation, with same, if not higher, degree of intensity. Thus, poverty perpetuates itself across generations.

The urgency, with which the poor had to engage in economically gainful work, leaves very little room for respite and lay off. Any breaks or off-days instantly plunges the individual into even more distressing conditions. This is why disease and illness is intensely dreaded among the poor. In poor people's lives it is not only the condition of illness and diseases that throw them into poverty, but the investment in health care made in returning the body to its working condition. In fact, the occasions at which heavy investment is made in medical care stand out as the watershed in the lives of poor - watershed for it is the point at which many poor families become poorer. The long period of illness or carrying disease means the loss of income for the person and the collectivities they belong to. Therefore, in their urge both to return to work at the earliest and economise on the expenses on health care, poor's indulgence in self-care is at best minimal and at worst nil. When some attempt is made at all in the direction of mitigating the wear and tear of the hard work, their choice of remedy is worse than disease it purports to cure. They use all sorts of toxicants and cheap drugs. The resultant degeneration caused to the body tends to shorten their life span, if not the span of healthy, efficient period.

There are many instances noticeable from the stories wherein the poor had to withdraw themselves from work life at such an early life, due to ill-health. This thereby inaugurates an era of poverty for the next generation, as it is compelled to take the baton from the worn and torn elders. Hence, we see many children jumping into woklife after being withdrawn from school at a much earlier stage. What is worse, the atrophying of the working members' bodies in ill- health is hurried up on account of the poor's involvement in hazardous work, like ragpicking, quarry work etc. Further adding pace to this are the living conditions of poor, both when they are at work and rest. These effect a forced withdrawal of the earning member from the worklife, endangering the survival of the family in the long run. Not alone this, the focussed energy of the dependent family members in bringing the ailing member back to worklife means, enormous strain on the women, as the primary responsibility for renewing the labour is placed on them. Withdrawal of children from school either for channelising the money for health care – the money lost and spent by sending the children to school -- or for attending to the needs of the sick member and selling off the residual asset are the recurring scenarios in poor's lives. This engineers the onset of extreme poverty in the family.

The position of women in the whole array of condition elaborated above is very precarious and atrociously unequal. Once the gender dimension is added to it, the impoverishment process gets doubly intensified and accelerated. Forced to engage in both the reproduction of labourers – the working bodies in the form of children, and the production of labour -- the working body of herself, and coming under the heavy load of traditional and religious expectations and stereotypes, she bears the burnt of impoverishment in all its multitudinal dimensions. She is expected to produce more children, as per the family expectations, whereas she is compelled to produce fewer children as per the state's expectations, risking her health and life in both situations. She travels twice the length of distance on a given period of time both in pursuit of work and in search of water, firewood, grains and medical care for her children, or even credit. She foregoes privileges, including education. At the time of economic crisis, she is denied even food while the male members may still be provided. She is forced to enter into worklife, both in reproduction and in production, earlier than her male counterparts. She is withdrawn from public sphere and confined to private spheres wherein she has to engage in economically gainful work, apart from her reproductive functions – reproduction of labourers and labour so that it is readied for next day's circulation. Unfortunately, neither of these is valued significantly. She atrophies faster than the menfolk, for she is doubly distressed all through due to the compulsions to renew her labouring potency. This she performs under the limitation imposed by tradition and religion, which make it mandatory on her to beget and ready the male members for next day's work, even while she has none to attend to her health needs when stuck by illness. It is exactly because she is only eligible for self-care that she faces health risks, for only lesser or no investment is permitted to be made in her health. In old age too she is forced to work hard and to die unmourned. If resorting to trade off body and its raw resources for survival is the condition of poverty, women stands as the impoverished section of the poor. The crudest expression of this condition is the need to sell off her body for survival in sexwork. It has come to characterise the life of even some young boys who engage in sex work as male prostitutes.

Family as an agent and victim of impoverisation

The fundamental principal upon which the whole edifice of deprivation and denial which exacerbates poverty has been erected, is the body-dependent existence that poor are forced to resort to. It is also the hypothetical starting point in the perimeter of the vicious cycle set in motion by interplay of various forces operating at different levels of proximity to poor. Family thus occupies an important place both as an impoverishing force as well as the terrain on which impoverishing processes are played out in full intensity, despite the potential of the family to offer buffer against these. In recent years, as the stories bear testimony, family has come under increasing stress and gradually cracking, while losing many of the cushioning function it performed against the harsh outer world. Now the emerging realities not only have made the wall of the family weak but also permeable to the exploitative forces extraneous to it, thereby a mere extension of the impoverishing forces. As a matter of fact, the impoverishing nature of the family is the last residual quality that has always persisted with family across time and space amidst all other tendencies within it to moderate the full play of this.

This is what stands out in the stories we have collected. There are two trends clearly visible: one family has been dissolving gradually in the recent past of the poor, hence throwing its members to the impoverishing conditions of the harsh public sphere upfront; secondly, family has come to retain the only residual impoverishing and exploitative quality, thus turning itself into an impoverishing force in its own right. These trends exist despite sporadic yet unsuccessful attempt by its members to reclaim its cushioning functions, either by reorganising it into joint-families

Co-opted by the exploitative economic logic of the public sphere, even while getting simultaneously rendered fragile by it, the families of poor in contemporary times accelerate the processes of reducing their members to body-dependent survivors. This they do also as carriers and guardians of traditional values, of which patriarchy assumes enormous importance. In poor persons' lives the circulation of poverty to the next generation is activated through the family. It is the family which gives least importance to human investment made in the forms of education and acquisition of other cultural capital. It is the family which inaugurates the period of harsh labour for the young ones. It is family which socialises its future members into a life in poverty by normalising body-dependent survival, so much so that childhood spent without gainful work is treated as idle phase of life. We even come across 10 year old boy talking about discharging family responsibility and sharing the burden of family through, essentially, the use of his body and its raw resources.

It is family as a carrier of tradition that devalues contribution made by its women members. It is family that initiates women's entry into the world of work that goes unrewarded and grossly undervalued. A female child enters into worklife much earlier than the male children. She also gets initiated into reproductive work once she attains puberty, for the family values the arrival of new workforce in the form of children. That no investment is made in her skills and capacities both during her stay in the family of birth as well as in the family of marriage renders her totally incapable of overcoming her poverty in all its forms. If anything, her marriage heralds an end of new investment in her skills forever.

The organisation of gainful work around the male-head of the family has tragic consequences. Because the lion's share of the investment, for keeping the raw resources of the body in working condition in order that it may be available for trading in the market situation, is made only for male members of the family, and the male head at that, their sudden demise or disloyalty to the family endangers the very continuity of the family. It throws the family into utter poverty. Primarily the cause being least or no investment made in skills and capacities of other family members, previous to the death or disloyalty of the male head. That is why we see the return of the women to economically under-rewarding yet physically exhausting works they did several years ago as members of the natal family. The centring of gainful work around the male head has even more cascading effect: Once male head's presence is not there permanently, the family migrates to newer places for work and survive in excruciating conditions of assetlessness - both social and economic - anonymity and insecurity. Subsequently the family circulates other members of the family, at whatever age they are in, in the market for gainful work. Summarily women and children face increased range of vulnerabilities and abuse.

Though comparative data not available, going by the generational differences observable in the stories, it is evident that more number of families lose men, who are the central breadwinners of the families, than they did in the previous generations, either in death or in withdrawal of their loyalty to the family. Various forces are at play in attenuating the ties that people had towards their families. Now we see more sons deserting the families of their birth, more husbands abandoning their wives and more brothers refusing to assist their sibling. The heavy burden of nurturing the children and siblings falls on the shoulders of the women who were least readied for it by the conspiracy of the patriarchy. In the hostile world of work, women, thus, suffer the most. Unable to cope with the demands of the rugged public sphere and harsh expectations of the families they belong to, many women find themselves in streets, prisons, brothel areas and mental asylums.

The hallmark of the successful cooption of family into the exploitative logic of the contemporary society is the hostility shown towards its disabled members of the family, whereas their disability itself is the result of lowest investment it made both in the mother's health throughout and the child's health after its birth. The family adds insult to injury of the disabled child by treating it as a burden and a threat to the very survival of the family. This domestic hostility and devaluation, combined with the public hostility, impoverishes the disabled members at twice the intensity with which it does for the abled ones. Thus, the disabled members are, at best, made to toil with all their physical limitation to prove their economic worth or, at worst, detested, unwanted, uncared and allowed to die underfed. If the disabled person is so physically infirm to do any physical work, the compulsion to find economic worth does not still abate. Such persons are also forced to resort to using body as a resource for survival. Perhaps in their cases, the body is the sympathy-generating resource used when engaged in begging. There are instances in which the family members themselves encourage the disabled person to enter into begging. The same fate befalls on the aged population too. In their old age, it is the atrophied and worn-out body that becomes the sympathy-evoking resource for the beggars.

In the effort to renew the labouring potency of the working members, not only the women members of the family take part but also the children, particularly female children. The moment the female child is forced to care for the newborn siblings, the script is written for the future poverty of the female children, who drop out of education or any other capacity building opportunities and also get their mobility severely limited.

If family is an impoverishing force in the newly-arriving circumstances, it is not because of the tendencies intrinsic to it, though some elements of that are present, but because it has come to mediate impoverishing conditions in an uncritical and unchecked manner. Whatever the checks and balances possessed by the family, which softened the shocks and jolts created by the forces external to it, have withered away due to the increasing stress the family has come under in recent years. Till recently, the family had assumed many roles and responsibilities. The most significant of them are:

1. the economic security it offered to its members in times of unemployment
2. the involvement of its young members in skill-building
3. the health care and attention it gave to its sick members through the use of indigenous medical wisdom strengthened by the matching ecology filled with flora and fauna specific to that medical wisdom
4. The long period of apprenticeship it provided to its younger members in acquisition of skill specific to the family, such as pot making, basket weaving, carpentry etc. These skills had an assured clientele, thus giving room for improvisation and excellence for increasing economic resources.
5. It gave psychological security to its members by ensuring a readily available collective strength derived from geographically proximate kin groups.

All these functions, however gender discriminatory they are, have been purportedly substituted by a new set of institutions, whose reach and access remain elusive to the poor. In its vengeful search for relevance, the family has retained only the impoverishing functions and perpetuates only exploitative conditions. This is further worsened by the gradual blurring and seamless suturing of its border with the outside world, whose exploitative potency need no elaboration. Though we see incidences of poor people striving to re-establish family in its classic joint family lines to counter the impoverishing forces, they are failing for this occurs in the absence of radical reorganisation of society at large.

Community to neighbourhood: The great transition

Contemporary collective life, as the stories make abundantly clear, is characterised by the dissolution of communities, for right and wrong reasons, and the arrival of neighbourhoods. This process generates severe shocks and offer cruel challenges for every one who gets caught in it. With market forces making capital out of this transition by offering cost-specified solutions and services to overcome the debilitating effects produced by this transition, only the rich and moneyed could escape from the onslaught. The poor remain gravely affected by it and are steadily rendered poorer, both in absolute terms, because they are losing whatever little assets and resources they have, therefore unable to purchase the commoditised solution and services; and in comparative terms because they perceive themselves more and more deprived.

The negative evaluation of the emergence of neighbourhood as the dominant expression of collective living, though, does not absolve communities of their exploitative, discriminatory and impoverishing potentials. In spite of all the hardships and insecurity experienced in urban centres, the poor find these places less harsh than the communities to which they belong, be it village or religious. The excessively discriminatory attitude that communities evince and the intense hostility they show for the courageous members who have violated the community norms, make life in neighbourhood more manageable and bearable. Particularly the remnants of feudalism and feudal delivery of justice in village communities have engineered terrible forms of denial, deprivation and damage to the poor. Its naked extortion of poor people's labour in the form of bonded labour, its cruel refusal of justice to the wronged poor and its overt discrimination of the poor, have made the faceless life in new places a much more bearable experience. This is more so in the case of women who are severely impoverished under feudal condition as well as any condition where traditional and religious hold is very strong. Even at the height of their frustration with traditional institutions including families, they could scarcely afford to escape from them with the hope of living alone in the hostile male dominated world. A lonely woman is frowned upon and subjected to undue hardships. Therefore, women seek asylums in many total institutions such as prison, asylums and orphanages that are relatively free from the grip of traditions or religions. In a manner of speaking, these total institutions offer the desired non-institutional spaces where women feel less vulnerable, albeit their intrinsically dehumanising character. In women's perception the insensitivity and unresponsiveness of the traditional or religious communities to their aspirations render the non-institutional spaces such as prison, asylum etc. more inhabitable. Women are frustrated with the stigmatising, depriving and denying traditional social spaces.

What one observes in the massive circulation of poor in motion is the increasing incidence of poor people living in completely unfamiliar places - places not their own birth enters, places bereft of communitarian ties and places where none takes responsibility for another persons' life. The heightened scale of mobility of the poor in search of work opportunities takes them to newer places, surround by people who speak different languages, think different thoughts, eat different food, and follow different cultural styles and religions. These outlandish locales offer least or no psychological security and are filled with people who, at best, remain indifferent or, at worst, pose threat. There is no assistance available as an expression of moral commitment to each others well-being. If it ever comes, it is out of contractual obligation, maybe for the work performed or service rendered. The poor discover, all of a sudden, that what was available freely in their village community, now has a cost attached to it - from water to psychological comfort.

The arrival of the poor to these neighbourhoods in urban centres, as well as in places not their own, is marked by preceding conditions poverty in their pre-migrant locations. Consequently, the poor find themselves severely distressed and impoverished by these new circumstances. They find themselves pushed to make residence out of places abandoned and shunned by the privileged and rich. Thus, we find poor living in the banks of sewer canals, in areas bordering dumping grounds for industrial wastes or garbage and in other hazardous locations. Surrounding them is vast sea of population which may be different from one another in every respect, excepting their impoverished existence. In rural areas, poor occupy spaces untouched or abused by developmental process, such as submerged areas near dams, polluted areas near factories etc. In both types of places, prevails a distinct culture of poverty that perpetuates inbreeding of poverty either in its existing forms or in cruder and crueler forms.

Culture of Poverty

The poor, hemmed in by similarly-destined people in their immediate vicinity, find themselves forced by the uniquely common culture that can be characterised as the culture of poverty. This is both a product and producer of circumstances into which poor have been forced to live. While the culture of poverty is more commonly observable in the lives of poor in urban centres, the elements of the same could be found in rural areas wherein the traditions and customs specific to each community engender the same impoverishing tendencies. In the rural culture of poverty, the hold of the traditional worldview and religious tenets is so tight that it produces equally discriminatory, exploitative and debilitative effects upon its members.

The culture of poverty has beliefs, attitudes and behaviours very different from the rest/ mainstream culture. This culture of poverty is developed from the poor's common experiences of sole use of physical labour and continual labouring for survival. This common experience of an individual brings out certain survival tactics in them. When the individual find that the same survival tactics are being followed by others in the neighbourhood, their beliefs on those survival tactics get strong. This way, the common believes, which are reinforced among the individuals, become a culture, very different from the mainstream culture. Not strangely, this culture of poverty plays a major role in keeping the poor inside the vicious circle of poverty.

Appreciation of the use of raw physical labour for self survival: In the culture of poverty, family does not act as buffer on which the individuals can depend. The culture sees the use of raw physical labour to satisfy ones need, as an essential trait and any dependence on other individuals in a family is not appreciated. A state where raw labour is not used is considered to be idle and useless.

This culture does not even discriminate between different age group. Therefore people in no age group are expected to live without using their raw physical labour. As soon as the child starts its childhood, it is given apprentice in doing work at home and soon it is sent out to earn.

The childhood, in this culture, is seen as an idle period, if not characterised by and spent in gainful work. Thus, the inbreeding of poverty occurs when the poor socialises the next generation into menial, impoverishing works, ensuring continuation of their poverty, throughout life. The society talks about the responsibility of the child in easing the family burden – taking away his burden from the family- and the desire for education is treated as irresponsible dream. Even the aspiration level of the children has a ceiling imposed by the culture of poverty. At most they aspire to become a maid servant when they grow up.

This appreciation – expectation – of raw physical labour for self survival, many a times has very brutal face. It makes the women labour hard even during pregnancies and soon after their child birth. The women who can withstand such work without much are praised by this culture as strong. Grown-up women apart, even the new born babies are put to use by renting them to beggars. For aged person, an early death while doing overburdened hard physical work is acceptable and decent, but old age dependencies are not permitted. The leaves no other options than culturally acceptable "use of raw labour" through beggary.

Survival is the only end: As discussed earlier, the first utilisation of raw resources of the body happens in childhood, in the culture of poverty. At this tender age, when the child is pushed into labour, he begins his association with the peripheral sector (away from the main stream market economy), which needs the use of raw labour. When the child joins this sector, it also joins the race for survival. Survival, being the only goal/end in this society, it appreciates the possibility of survival rather than means to achieve it. The culture does not care much about the means used to achieve the end. Thus, appreciation of attainment of end and indifference towards mean has led to legitimisation of stealing, beggary sexwork etc.

Take the case of begging, the culture of poverty treats it as normal. It normalises begging to the extent that tactful begging is appreciated and often solicited. It is common to find beggars taking babies for rent and wrapping bandages with red colour, to arouse sympathy among people. This type of tactfulness is greatly appreciated by family and neighbours.

The sheer indifference towards means in this culture has encouraged many children to stealing at very early stages and the entry into sexwork soon after the girl attains puberty.

The culture of poverty has also blurred the difference between educated and uneducated, in this society. It is not being educated which is appreciated but it is the attainment of survival which matters most.

The culture which appreciates the learning of these survival instincts at very early age has also blurred the age differences. As the child is not left unexposed to the harsh realities of the fight of survival, it transits into adult at a very early age (mostly at the age of 10). Even certain kinds of wisdoms about of sex work, body as saleable unit etc, are learned by child at a very early age.

The risky and threat-filled world of the poor does not place high premium of saving money in excess, perhaps possible for sexworkers and beggars among them. That the beggar will be stripped of theirs excess money by the rogues and even the police or that sexworkers will have to part with their money to the dons controlling their areas or to the police or to the irresponsible and drunken husbands or fathers, discourage them from saving their excess money. They rather squander it on non-essentials like cosmetics, sweets, movies etc than saving it and losing it. This only triggers the cycle of poverty as they have to seek the help of moneylenders at the time of crisis.

State: Resposible or Strong?

A journey through the life events of the poor repeatedly highlights the colossal failure, enormous callousness and wholesale irresponsibility of the State and its various agencies. This way the state can be characterised as the most important and central impoverishing force in the lives of poor. State can cause this by its indifference to, irresponsibility for and excessive intervention in the lives of poor. In fact, from the life events of the poor people's stories one could figure out the large extension of impoverisation having been caused by the irresponsibilities or misplaced responsibilities of the State. However, this only reiterates the fact that State can cause significant public good and positive impact on the poor if it becomes more responsible and places the same rightly through participatory and dialogical processes of planning, implementation and evaluation.

Particularly, in the lives of poor, its major manifestation of irresponsibility is the failure to adequately crate reliable and accessible structures that offer services and resources provided by the traditional ones. Indeed the very marginalisation and dissolutions of traditional structures such as family as the unit of production, feudal economy and its justice delivery mechanisms, caste based guilds that ensured apprenticeship for the young generation, religion centred medical practitioners etc. have been largely unaccompanied by replacement of alternative structures that are within the immediate reach of the poor, both spatially and temporally. State is a definite and most important party to legitimise and accelerate this transition – traditional structures to modern structures. With the State's active involvement, combining with other modernising forces, poor people's lives are radically reorganised. Poor people are now bearing witness to the disappearance of many familiar, intelligible and relatable traditional structures and their inbuilt functions, albeit their having the tendency to discriminate and exploit. We have elaborated about the transformation happening to family and community. Similarly, many other structures and function legitimised by tradition and religion are fast receding in the background and getting erased eventually from the lives and memories of the people at large.

The poor are the worst affected though. While they are relieved by the declining importance of the traditional forces that held exploitative rather than emancipatory potency, they find themselves surrounded by the substituting the State- or market-created structures that are fewer in number than what is needed to make poor people's lives better. Moreover, these modern institutions are mostly inaccessible due to their intrinsic hostility traditional wisdom. They are amenable only to those who subject themselves to their certification of eligibility. They also hold highly prohibitive hidden costs to be paid for using them both in terms of the money spent on the travel to reach them and the money to oil the palms of the corrupt officials in them. What is even more alarming in the contemporary context is the assumption of the brokering role that the State is playing by permitting the market to take over the very structures and institutions once constructed by the State after replacing or appropriating the traditional institutions and their functions. We shall dwell on this later in the section on market.

Another form of irresponsibility of the State is the misplaced responsibility of the State, which is equally impoverishing, if not more. Arising out of the arrogance of scientific and expert wisdom unabashedly legitimised by modern institutions, is the unilateral responsibility that the State has taken to better the lives of the poor. Backed by least or no sensitivity to design its responsibility in tune with the felt-needs of the poor, the State imposes its will on the people in ways that defeat their very intentions. Here one can recall development initiatives like dam building, credit facilities, industrialisation, forest management, ecological management and land reforms. These have far more serious impoverishing consequences for the poor.

It has been already elaborated as to how a complex of forces, not the least of which being the State, has pushed the poor to become poorer by forcing them to depend increasingly on their bodies and their raw resources for survival. Thus, the poor earn far less than what could be required to renew themselves for next day's work, if ever it is available. Already in possession of negligible resources, the poor are further deprived of the services, such as health, credit, justice and apprenticeships in family occupations etc., provided by the traditional institutions, subsequent to the arrival of the modern State. The compulsions to seek the same services from the externalised institutions like hospitals, educational institutions, court and banks along with the high hidden costs to be paid in availing them has rendered the poor poorer both in absolute and comparative terms. Absolute, because they are deprived of the services in the given circumstances, they find themselves in and also because they can never afford to access these services without impoverishing themselves for the heavy costs demanded by them. Comparatively, because power and resourcefulness are measured in terms of easy access and control over these institutions, the poor have been driven to perceive themselves as poorer by their own standards in comparison to the non-poor.

The easy access to the portals of the modern institutions and their services is extremely difficult for the poor because they are far away geographically, requiring investment of time and money to cross the distances. The poor could hardly afford to risk their day's income for having to travel to these places, mostly urban centres. But this is only one side of the coin, on the other side is the mastery that the poor have to, perforce, develop over the whole array of practices and knowledge system privileged and legitimised by the State and other modern institutions to avail their services. This happens as a two-step process. First the poor persons' wisdom, capacities and experiences stand severely discredited by these modern institutions, thereby forcing the poor to acquire them all over again in forms validated by the modern forces. But this requires intense investment of long period of time and fair amount of money spent in educational institutions, training programmes and other industrial work spheres in the "economically unrewarding capacity" of a student and an apprentice. This is highly unthinkable for the poor who shudder to lose the income generated by their working bodies, which have to be continuously exerted for survival. Thus, the poor find themselves gradually excluded from these institutions and consequently from enjoying their services. They, therefore, resort to "short-cut" wisdoms, capacities and solutions that not only stand discredited but also criminalised. Here one may recall wider prevalence of drug addiction, beggary, theft, sex work, thuggery, extortionary arbitration overseen by goondas etc.

In those rare circumstances in which the poor eventually seek the services of the modern institutions, by no means out of any desire for fair justice and any sense of right, but out of sheer desperation for survival, they end up devastated and irrevocably impoverished for their courageous acts. Those occasions of courageous encounters with the modern institutions are the first and final fall into the abyss of poverty. This is stunningly true in the case of health care and justice delivery institutions, namely hospitals and court. These two services have been largely appropriated from the very lifeworlds of the people and locked in a modified and neutralised form in the cloisters of hospitals and courts.

Health Care: Take the case of health care. The progressive irresponsibility of the State has resulted in limited reach of the health care to the poor, on the one hand and increasing hidden and visible costs further multiplied by the swelling of privatised health care, on the other. In fact it is the State which has quietly and tacitly permitted private health care systems to take over the spaces evacuated of traditional health care facilities and later vacated by the State's own institutions of health care. Now for any serious illness and severe diseases the poor have to depend on private health care facilities, for there is a clear evidence of State's wholesale failure in providing quality health care. These private health care services are offered at highly prohibitive price.

It is a fact that the poor are becoming increasingly prone to serious illness due to low investment in well-being and their continuing to live and work in extremely polluting and hazardous situations. The breakdown of body rhythms, because of illness or diseases, is deeply dreaded by the poor, for the cumulative economic loss it causes. To cut costs, they take recourse to consulting quacks, purchasing medicines across the counters of drugstores, where the seller double up as poor people's physician or getting themselves addicted to drugs, liquor, pan chewing etc., to mitigate the pain and the fatigue. Only when things come to a head, they resort to professional medical services now offered "better" only in private establishments. The exorbitant fees they pay render them either assetless, if at all they have assets, or bonded to moneylenders. Whether one likes it or not, poor people are strongly distrustful of and disappointed with public health systems.

Justice Systems: Now let us look at the courts. The poor are increasingly forced to seek justice mostly through modern agencies like police and court. Not only do these institutions remain heavily removed from the mental horizons of the people but also from their geographical horizons. These institutions and the whole surfeit of practices they unleashed where grafted on to the traditional social structures after de-legitimising their deeply entrenched practises. But the continuation of the traditional behavioural patterns and styles of relationship-building persist in the interstices of the modern institutions, thereby creating corrupt practices. Here references are made to gift giving, treating discharge of official duty as demonstration of benevolence and munificence and so on and so forth. Once corrupt practices entrench themselves in, the hidden costs to avail the services of these institutions spiral. Worse still, are the visible costs to be paid to the lawyer and to the whole lot of paraphernalia. Thus, these institutions become distanced from the reach of the poor. Their woes are further aggravated by the demand that these institutions place on the poor to possess the whole lot of capacities, resources, lateral awareness, certified proofs etc. The poor are largely illiterate, mostly unaware of legal nuances, not known to persons in these institutions who can take responsibility for getting justice and do not possess whole lot of documentary evidences and certificates to make any sense to these institutions. Thus, the poor shun these institutions, for the impoverishing effects they have on them. But in the absence of any other means to seek justice, their vulnerabilities to the exploitative, forces lurking around them only get multiplied.

Particularly women are the doubly-distressed section of the poor. The poor-excluding stature of these institutions unwittingly or wittingly conspires with the patriarchy to force the women to accept their victimhood forever. Their vulnerabilities are on the rise, when they rail against their perpetual victimisation. They are punished severely by patriarchy whose agent the State and its institutions have became willy-nilly, perhaps inadvertently in places like India and Vietnam, but blatantly in Pakistan, Bangaldesh and Nepal. In the latter one sees the States' complicit relationship with religion and tradition.

If some among the poor are talking nostalgically about the past or communication life or village environs, it is an indication of the overall failure of the State to create alternative structures, more humane and liberating than that of the traditional structures it replaced. If poor are spending vengefully more money on marriages, funerals and other collective rituals, celebrations ceremonies and festivals, than perhaps on health, or justice or education, it only speaks voluminously of their desire to build collectivities based on trust and mutual dependence. This is their time-honoured way of insuring themselves against external aggression (sometimes even from the State itself). The poor are resort to doing what they have always been doing - strengthening social assets, like collectivities that come to their rescue at the times of crises.

The whole repertoire of skills and capacities with which to deal with the state, and a series of disciplining to which they have to subject themselves, so as to appear respectable and sensible to get the State services, have repelled the poor to take to earlier forms of collectivities like caste, ethnic groups. Curiously, by comparison they begin to appear more humane and responsive to their needs. This is starkly evidenced in what has occurred when poor deal with credit-providing institutions like bank or co-operative society. In these places the insensitive demands for collaterals, documents in proof of residence, citizenship, death of the family members, loss of property in natural disasters etc. consume a lot of time, apart from forcing them to deal with corrupt, insensitive subsidiary wings of the State like panchayat office, village development committee, disability rehabilitation officer etc. In contrast, the poor find the local moneylender's readiness to give the needed money without all these foot-dragging requirements a humane, timely and responsive gesture, albeit the crushing interest rate levied upon the capital.

The above are instances of State's irresponsibility. Even when the State acts responsibly, but without taking in account what kind of responsibility that people want to see in it, it can cause impoverisation of the poor. Since the responsibility of the State is defined under the shadow of rational scientific worldview, it tends have homogenising and insensitively equalising effects. The forced displacement of people from the places of their birth to what the State defines as development zones, industrial belts, new-economic zones etc., causes enormous amount of hardships to the poor, for they find their traditional context-specific skills and capacities unwanted and obsolete in the new contexts. But for the modern State both the places are equalisable and identical. Similarly when it builds massive infrastructure like dams, roads and industries, ostensibly for the welfare of the poor, they have more often than not produced negative consequences. But the State does not pay proper compensation to the poor. Even if it is paid, it is linked to certification regimes, forcing the poor to exclude themselves from the beneficiaries list, for they lack the facility to enter into confident negotiations.

On another count too the impoverisation processes set off by the State because of its discharging of mis-placed responsibility becomes evident. It is in the sphere of ecological management. Before the State has been forced to adhere to global environmental standard regimes, the wider disregard for environmental standards in the respective countries caused untrammeled pollution and contamination of natural resources. The poor were the most affected as they were exposed to pollution, both as innocent residents in houses located in the banks of canal turned into sewage by the industrial effluence, near the dumping yards where the garbage generated by non-poor's avaricious consumption habits are heaped and on the roadsides as pavement dwellers breathing the automobile emissions, and also as unofficial protectors through the cleaning work they do as rag pickers, as auto rickshaw and manual rickshaw drivers (the latter swiftly transport the non-poor through these zones even while they themselves make a living in these places day in and day out exposing themselves to the hazards).

Nobody pays compensation to the poor in any form whatsoever for not only being forced to live in the pollution zones but also for the protection they offer to the wider society. So much for the irresponsibility of the state. But what happens to poor, when the State gets suddenly woken up to adherence to environmental standards, itself is a tragic story. The moment environmental standards are promulgated, it is the poor who get driven out of their living spaces, whose means of survival like rickshaws, and other implements are seized, and who loses job in the factories closed for violation of such specified standards. So much for the responsibility of the state.

In spite of all the frustration and distrust, people in the stories view the State with an optimism not reserved even for some of the traditional institutions that have grown with them for generations. It is just that they want the state to become a responsible force - responsibility tempered with participatory spirit. But even while the plea for the arrival of responsible State is aired, one sees the emergence of an ominously strong State. The local and international terrorism/extremism and national and civil war have spurred the State to militarise itself and the various territories within its boundaries. The worst affected are the poor again. It is they who lose easy access to forest areas where they collected their survival resources and grazed their livestock, it is the poor who are being compelled to travel long distances circumventing terrorism-prone zones, and it is they who come under criminalising influences due to the presence of police and terrorists in the zones close by.

Market and Globalisation

The increasing presence of market forces now unfettered by a watchdog State has more impoverishing consequences than ever. While the state gradually receded from the public sphere shrinking its range of responsibilities to the welfare of its citizens, it has left many traditional institutions totally corroded in its wake. The market forces have come to occupy the zones vacated by the State. Thus, an unbridled commoditisation and commercialisation of welfare services is in order. The poor are forced to *purchase or perish* (ironically, in poor persons' lives it is *purchase and perish*).

Market forces joining hands with globalisation forces, more particularly information and communication technologies have further privileged knowledge- and information-encoded work as the only valid form of gainful activity. The labour thus has become embedded with knowledge and information. In the era of knowledge workers heralded by the information technology revolution, the contours, content, and relevance of knowledge and information transform at a rapid pace and today's knowledge renders yesterday's knowledge obsolete. So only those workers who are engaged in continual renewal of, not onlytheir labouring *body*, but also the labouring *mind* could survive. Not only is one forced to earn enough to keep the body ready for next days' work but also the mind. But renewal of knowledge to become eligible for next day's work is a costly proposition. But the new knowledge package is not derivative of the work experience gathered in the work spheres. If it is so, it would have demanded no investment of time and money outside of the work engaged in. The new knowledge-package is essentially disengaged from workplaces and manufactured in the research and development wings of the few monopoly companies, which disseminate the knowledge-package through their franchise agencies across the globe. Equipping one with new knowledge package, needs lots of money and spare time. Therefore, even the privileged knowledge workers have to invest huge amount for continual renewal of their minds and live in constant fear of falling behind and subsequently lay off.

One can easily imagine the plight of the poor. Already unwanted and underpaid by an economy that placed at least some premium on raw physical labour, the poor is bound to find themselves rejected both in the core and periphery of the market. Since even the most peripheral of the economically gainful activities being embedded with knowledge and information, the poor will be forced to transact only with the shadow regions of the market such as sanitation work, garbage removal etc. but this is only a transitory phenomenon. The greedy nature of the market will soon envelop even these shadow regions and embed them with knowledge and information, forcing the poor to conduct transactions elsewhere, if ever there is an 'elsewhere'. If some of the stories are any indication, one day the poor will find their raw bodily resources absolutely unpurchased by and intransactable in any region of the market. At that juncture, it is the body itself that will have to be sold or perilously risked for survival. Now more poor women are forced to become sex workers, at a much earlier stage in their lives than before. We have girls who enter into sex work covertly even before attending puberty. Even young boys become male prostitutes. Men, even some women, take to crime at a faster rate and higher frequency than before, risking corporal punishments. Body using, body selling, and body risking are the only ways out available to poor and strictly in that order only.

IX

Understanding Governance and Researching Our Way Out of Poverty

<u>THE DETERIORATING HUMAN CONDITION</u>

In the development literature, human existence and relating (being) - has been given poor priority when compared to task-based delivery of outputs (becoming). This has entailed a fragmented, instrumentalised and result-oriented understanding of human lives, further resulting in increasing isolation and exclusion of people from processes that govern their lives. These processes have acquired virulent intensity particularly in past 60 years, since 1949 when the era of development is said to have begun (Sachs 1992). It is during this time, that many modern institutions with their authoring power on people's lives have consolidated their tremendous power in the hands of a small section of the elite for achieving their self-serving purpose (Parasuraman, et.al. 2004).

This consolidation and rising power of modern institutions has coincided with intensification of processes that have radically transformed the very nature of people's traditional institutions that were proximal to their lives such as families and communities. In many instances, these traditional institutions have been torn apart, progressively discredited or rendered irrelevant. This has in turn ruptured the inter-relatedness between people and their environment. On their part , traditional institutions, in reaction to the challenge to survive, have mostly reacted by polarising rank and privilege within, and strengthening their exploitative and discriminatory functions.

The role of modern institutions in exacerbating the deterioration of the lives of the vast sections of the population has to be elaborated. Indeed the reason for the deteriorating human condition is that increasingly powerful modern institutions [state and market] are becoming indifferent to the human well-being. These institutions based as they are on rational western science and its Cartesian dualistic philosophy, characterise human experience as mechanised systems and reduce people to machines. They often aim at short-sighted economic gain and are fuelled by vast advances in technology. In their single – minded quest for profit and efficiency, these institutions have reduced more and more people across the globe to their labouring bodies and have excluded them from decisions that determine their lives.

Hence in the last few decades, the intensity of exploitative and exclusionary processes encoded within human institutions has been aggravated. For most part, both kinds of these institutions [traditional and modern] have disempowered people and communities and failed to meet their self-actualisation needs and collective well-being goals of their members.

FRAGMENTATION OF TRADITIONAL INSTITUTIONS

The most proximal institutions historically for people have been traditional ones such as family, clan and community. Individual belonging and collective well-being are critical concerns of these institutions. Many of these traditional institutions are built on holistic perspectives that recognise the inter-relatedness of human existence with each other and their environment.

Historically, traditional institutions played several roles based on this holistic perspective: governance of people's commons; grievance redressal, conflict resolution and justice; nurturance and social security of members, particularly the very young and the very old; economic production, such as caste-based guilds that had patronage and apprenticed members for training; indigenous medicinal and engineering practices; spirituality, philosophy and religion.

However, it is equally true that in more instances, traditional institutions allot hierarchical rank and privilege and rigid roles to their members; and are authoritarian and discriminatory [along gender, age, ethnicity, ability, caste and race lines]. Their very emphasis on relatedness often resulted in pervasive exploitative behaviours in all the aspects of individual experience. Because many of these traditional institutions valued collective well-being, they often accord individual self-actualisation needs secondary status, particularly for those with lower rank and privilege. The repercussions on those who did not adhere to their prescribed rank and roles within these hierarchies or transgressed institutional norms are severe.

The second core element in these institutions is the relationship that these communities share with their environment. Communities, traditionally, have been often defined by geographical proximity, embedded in their natural eco-systems. Since the beginning of civilization, local communities have claimed adjacent ecological resources, both land and sea. Communities understand their role as stewards of these eco-systems; and often institute a relationship based on respect in their governance of these resources. Their relations were, for most part, in keeping with naturally occurring historical patterns and in alignment with the other parts of the systems. These were based on sustainable and equitable usufractory rights.

Finally, threatened by the rapid pace of change and the ethical requirements to manage it, traditional institutions resort to rigid adherence of the most "literal" traditional values and meanings usually encoded in scripture or through orthodox practices to determine their values. These values often emphasise hierarchical rank and privilege within these institutions. Members who are historically powerful within these institutions managed to buffer and utilise modern processes for self-serving purposes and often augment their positions of power. Traditional institutions are also no longer able or are unwilling to provide the relatedness and care that they did previously. Those that have been historically disempowered in these institutions - women, children, old people, the differently abled, ethnic, race and castes hierarchies – have been further exploited or completely excluded.

DEHUMANISATION OF PEOPLE

"The history that affects every man is world history."[i]

In the last few decades, Modern Technology and Institutions have engineered foundational changes in human lives; rapidly and relentlessly restructuring them, their purpose and how they relate to each other and their environment. Simultaneously, a vast array of institutional formations that span the globe have emerged; ranging from global governance bodies, particularly economic governance, to the nation-state to common interest groups. Often this restructuring of people's lives has dehumanised vast majority among, them, reducing them to their labouring bodies, machine like and dispensable.

Modern science, upon which the edifice of modern institutions is built, reduces human collectivity and institutions to engineering models and characterizes human processes as goal-directed endeavours to enhance material well-being in any one single direction in logical, linear, repeatable and planned order based on a distinctly identifiable set of cause and effect variables. In this reduction, modern science systemically denies the intelligent, self-organising and emergent nature of living systems. It also reductively characterises human beings as machines engaged in mechanical action repeatedly; homogenised and deployed inter-changeably through the use of conceptual devices such as consumers, social capital, vote banks, labour pools.

This simplified conception of collectivism based on enumeration denies the human endeavour to seek balance between individual aspirations and accountability for collective human well-being (Dreze and Sen 1999). Hence, modern institutions have stopped moulding their members into critical citizens; instead emphasising uniformity and conformity. In their conception of resource sharing and justice, modern institutions apparently emphasise objectivity, fraternity and equality. In their claim of equality; they do not acknowledge differences of individual rank and privilege. Self-determination [survival and success] is attributed to personal competence; and failure to succeed is a result of personal inadequacy.

It must be stated clearly that modern institutions themselves do not articulate an exploitative position overtly, and indeed might publicly claim to be participative and empowering. They do not take cognisance of the fact that, their very prioritizing of objectivity and rationality over ethics and human experience and their lack of compassion for human well-being creates a "value" vacuum. This vacuum is rapidly occupied by the most powerful and often oppressive forces currently under play (Hannerz Ulf 1991). These forces tap into vast, emotional and repressed reservoirs of power and reintroduce truth for their self serving purposes. For instance, in modern India, there was a public denial of the importance diverse mythology in people's lives to understand their reality. This social denial has resulted in the homogenisation and manipulation of these powerful latent symbols by fundamentalist forces to incite violence and religious hatred across the nation.

These institutions also deny deeper issues of historical discrimination and inequity in which self-determination is embedded. They deny that the playing field on which people live their lives out is actually not a level one, but deeply contoured by history and experience. They refuse to also address it proactively, and tacitly permit, and even exacerbate exploitation and exclusion of many of its members. For instance, a Dalit child who is a first generation learner and a Brahmin child who is supported by educated parents to study are tested on the same parameters in modern school examinations; in spite of the historically powerful social institution of caste, that creates vastly different, inequitable life contexts for both children.

Modern institutions have conferred new forms of rank and privilege by confining their membership only to those who meet certain elitist entry criteria [education, task proficiency, urbanisation, networks] and are enumerated for entitlement. For instance, not only do modern institutions invalidate indigenous knowledge systems, they have created new entry criteria that require its members to acquire expertise in their own science and technology. Accessing this expertise requires power and resources, for instance, time and money to be educated or trained in modern, educational institutions. Those who can access these entitlements in modern institutions are often traditional elite with historical rank and privilege, who leverage power to compete in the new contexts. Hence they have increased and consolidated resources of a few elite, increasing the gap between resource rich and poor.

Those people who are not able to meet these entry criteria are considered useless and excluded by modern institutions. In traditional institutions, though deeply ridden by rank and privilege, human belonging is an important purpose. Hence these institutions were deeply concerned with inclusion and considered nurturance as an important function. For instance, the traditional Panchayats in India would only excommunicate a village member if all other forms of punishment (asking forgivance, fines) failed; and then too only progressively, first excluded from being a member of immediate collective in the village and then excluded from social interaction. The latter was considered to be an extreme measure. Modern institutions instead value instrumentality and efficiency. They are not concerned with inclusion; ruthlessly excluding and ignoring large numbers of people, if they are not useful. Between the rupturing fabrics of traditional institutions and the indifference of modern institutions, more and more people fall through the social security net.

In sum, modern institutions have increased the vulnerability that many people, who have been structurally disempowered, (Smith 2000) experience. Most people forced to be part of modern process feel increasingly unheard, alienated, used and lonely (Mehta 1990, Srinivasan TN 1998, Gilpin 2000).

THE EMERGENT CONSUMPTION BIAS OF THE STATE

The progressive exclusion of many by decreeing them as 'useless' is very much the characteristic of the modern society, but it has acquired more salience in the contemporary times. The society we live in can be characterized as one that is making a swift transition from *production-centered* citizenship to *consumption-centered* citizenship. The heightened obsession with consumption has deleterious consequences for large section of the population among the non-poor, with the aged, infirm, HIV-Infected and disabled among them being affected the most. This obsession has received further fillip in the globalization times with the state going all out to promote growth without distributive justice.

Producer to consumer

This is precisely nothing but echoing of what is happening at the global arena. At the global level the celebration of the untrammeled consumer has triggered off a process of elision of the poor from the moral horizon of the society. At the national level the consumerist bias in constructing the notion of an ideal citizen has compelled the members of the society to seek their personal significance and private salvation in being able to consume the goods available in the market place in an unrestrained and uninterrupted manner, with an immediacy not associated with the productivist bias of the previous era. (In contrast, the State with the productivist orientation enjoined its citizens to defer gratification and free themselves from the immediacy of need for indulgence by saving their surplus income. The citizen of the foregone era was a supreme producer). The immediacy of indulgence and consumption is possible only for those who have vantage position in the frontline of economy and perfect fitness to receive and enjoy the good and services. Since that which is enjoyable today may become obsolete tomorrow, one has no room for deferring gratification. One has to consume in the here and now as doing so *only* constitutes the essence of a good citizen and significant person with a control over his/her destiny simultaneously. The fitness to consume with a sense of urgency and a compulsion of immediacy has become a global obsession among the non-poor. One should be fit enough to receive the sensations given off by the market forces.

Contrarily, the ones who do not possess the 'fitness' have to lose visibility and cannot lay claim to all the privileges available with the State for its desirable citizens. What is more, the ones without fitness are pathologised, marginalized, rendered incomplete and made to feel unwanted. Converting this institutional image to a self-image of each citizen is successfully completed by the cosmetic and entertainment industries. The continual and compulsive foregrounding and privileging of citizen who is shown only in the capacity of a *consumer* with least references to his/her worklife, is an expression of the transition from production-centred economy to consumption-centred economy.

DESTRUCTION OF THE ENVIRONMENT AND THE COMMONS

Just as modern science reduces human systems to engineering models; it also reduces nature into mechanistic models. Rational, western science sees nature as something to be captured, exploited and commoditised. Hence modern institutions rationalise the exploitation of natural eco-systems by reducing them to measurable, material resources in their imagination of growth and development. Human development is reduced systemically to economic development, and nature to natural resources. These natural resources then can be governed centrally, extracted and used for short term monetary gains. This greed has destroyed non-renewable global natural resources and degraded eco-systems drastically across the globe.

In this process, modern institutions alienated local communities from their traditional habitats, and ignored their wisdom in husbanding these eco-systems. A pivotal factor in this alienation process of local communities is the shift in the notion of property in the governance of these habitats. To achieve this shift, modern institutions, particularly the State, raise the question "who governs the land and water?" Answering this question, they originally conceived nature as being a great wild void[ii] that no one owned or governed: trees and fish in the water and land. They assumed an ownership vacuum, resulting in "null" ownership. Since no one owned these resources, they could be accessed by all and the law of competition and capture prevailed.

At this point, the nation-state stepped into this "vacuum" and converted "null property" into public property by drawing administrative boundaries. This public property could then be governed and regulated in a "rational" and 'efficient' way. What this rationalisation process had completely overlooked was that all natural eco-systems did not have null ownership. Local communities had already claimed and governed the eco-systems as commons.

These administrative boundaries cut through community commons and converted them into public property. Once converted into public property, the State began to make available natural eco-systems for extraction, often in an attempt to "rationalise" their use for national development. In the process, often public property became equivalent to private property; and these eco-systems were made available to fuel economic globalisation, that in turn consolidated global resources in the hands of a few. Even as it is clearly evident that this process of consolidation only benefits a few at the cost of many, it has been justified using the economic "trickle down" theory, the belief that it would eventually trickle down to everyone.

In reality, this rationalisation process rapidly reduces natural environment to a resource base; expropriates communities' rights to govern their commons and habitats and hands it over to a few individuals for self-serving purposes. In the process, it has fragmented individual meaning making and maps, discredited people's lived wisdoms and rendered their fierce intelligence irrelevant.

In many instances, these extractive processes has left natural eco-systems ravaged, with communities no longer able to eke out a living from them. In other instances, communities have been displaced by powerful, competitive interests from their environments; or else they have been denied their rights of access and governance of these eco-systems. Since these local communities no longer have governance (tenure, usufractory) rights in managing these eco-systems; they have begun to invest less energy, time and money to manage these resources. In order to survive in an increasingly competitive world, they often adopt the same extractive tools that other competitors used, going against their traditional wisdom and disregarding the damage to their environment.

More people have been forced to migrate into alien and often urban habitats, resulting in communities now transiting into neighbourhoods (more impersonal and unconcerned). Geographical markers based on inter-relatedness with each other and with their environment are no irrelevant. The wisdom about their habitats is dismissed as unworthy, superstitious, wasteful, unscientific and/or irrational and is no longer useful in their new contexts based on cash economies. Historical, traditional knowledge systems - very different from western science and often more holistic have been erased or irrevocably damaged.

FAILURE OF THE NATION-STATE

For most part, the nation-state has failed in its governance and welfare functions; particularly for those who have been historically discriminated. Though the modern nation-state entered with promises of equality and prosperity for all its citizens, its actual performance on the ground has been disappointing in many instances. Fundamental to this failure is the narrowing of its purpose from citizen's welfare and justice to economic development.

Hence, it has not been able to address existing inequities, allowing traditional elite to retain their positions of authority and control for their personal benefit; while absolving them of their responsibilities.

The poor performance of the nation-state in fulfilling many of its citizen's aspirations has left a vacuum in governance; not just at the national levels but also at the international levels; resulting in adverse consequences such as weakening of international democratic efforts such as SAARC. This vacuum has been quickly filled by private capital forces and global credit groups– centrally the World Bank and the IMF whose central purpose is economic growth and profit, without any ethical responsibility towards human welfare.

This unhealthy confluence of interests between the modern democratic state and capital is driven by underlying western philosophical commonalities that reduce human well-being to economic development. This confluence of interests has resulted in the permeability of national boundaries; in consolidating capitals, opening markets and pooling labour. One, national boundaries, particularly of developing countries have allowed the extraction of natural resources, and movement and consolidation of economic resources into the hands of a global elite network spanning the world. These elite are also often the maximum consumers of a global economic and natural resources and therefore are seen as favourable to the well-being of the nation (Bauman 1998). Second, national boundaries have been made permeable so that local markets have been opened, pitching them against powerful global forces in unhealthy competition, often affecting local sustainability. Third, the permeability of national boundaries has allowed private capital to predatorily shift their operations across national boundaries in search of "cheap" labour and consolidation of labour pools, unprotected by state regulation and machinery (Jaeger 1994, Nayar 2000). The people in these labour pools are usually unorganised, work under exploitative conditions, with poor life and livelihood security, and vulnerable to distant forces over which they have little knowledge and no authority. This created unbridled commoditisation and commercialisation of human lives, beginning with the body and extending to all relations that people have.

This prioritisation of economic development has also resulted in the erosion of social security and social welfare function of the state. In a "free market", where success is determined by competition, social welfare measures [education, health, public distribution systems] are seen as barriers for development. These social security measures are instead reduced from citizenship entitlements to commodities that people have to pay for. The welfare state is gradually receding or forced to recede from the public sphere shrinking its range of responsibilities to merely those related to militarisation and autocratic control (Sheila Pelizzon & John Casparis 1996). With time, these repressive powers of the state also became increasingly evident; with the nation-state showing increasing intolerance for dissenting voices (Khor M 2000, Madeley J 1999, Strange S 1999).

The corrosion of traditional organizations and the receding welfare state has meant that the responsibility to ensuring human rights and social security is shifted from collective to the personal, individual and private realm. Often this is beyond the means of the individual. (Ritzer G 1993). As a result, more and more people are exploited and excluded. This calls for a critical inquiry into the highly individualised Human Rights Framework.

FAILURE TO ELIMINATE POVERTY

Increasing number of people is being impoverished at a rapid pace, hastened by economic globalisation processes. Human economic well-being or well-becoming is being pulled in two directions (Baulch and McCulloc, 1998). A vast majority of people in the globe only 'become' poorer from 'being' poor over time. Simultaneously, there is a significant minority 'becoming' richer from being rich on an everyday basis (Narayan et al, 2000a & 2000b). The gap between those who were powerful and those who were exploited or excluded has increased. But ignoring these dynamics, poverty discourses often focus only on economic poverty, without conveniently questioning the constructed nature of poverty.

ERADICATION OF THE POOR

Economic globalisation has concentrated power and resources in the hands of a few global elite. It has reduced many other people to their labouring bodies, interchangeable with machines. This reduction, along with heightened competition for existing natural and man-made resources, has resulted in rendering large numbers of people irrelevant and dispensable to the resourceful population. When these people, who are the poorest, are no longer able to generate enough resources for their own survival, they become expendable. With this, the emphasis of society shifts from eradicating poverty to eliminating the poor.

Underlying this shift in perspective is indifference, and the death of compassion and responsibility in the repertoire of emotions in the resourceful population towards the poor. Writing about the banishing and death of the poor but not that of the poverty, Bauman writes, "The rich who happen to be at the same time the resourceful and the powerful among the actors of the political scene do not need the poor either for the salvation of their souls or for staying rich and getting richer. The poor are not god's children on which to practice the redemption of charity. They are not the reserve army of labourer, which need to be groomed back into wealth production. They are not the consumers who would be tempted and cajoled into giving the lead to recovery [of the economy]. Whichever way you look at them the poor are not of use. (Bauman, 2002)

Nevertheless, hunger and poverty raise morally embarrassing questions and demand ethically redeemable positions from society. Many of these elite rich who reap the benefits of these impoverishing processes escape their responsibility by living in insulated enclaves, and cleansing their imagination and geography of the presence of the poor.

First, in response to the challenge raised by hunger and poverty, the resourceful population rationalize poverty by individualizing it; by making entitlements a consequence of individual choice and merit rather than systemic causes. Sometimes this merit is accumulated in previous birth through karma, sometimes it is acquired by hard work, and sometimes by being intelligent. The poor people deserve to be poor because they have committed sins in their previous lives, or are lazy or are stupid. By reducing poverty to a personal choice – 'the poor choose to be poor', they evade the embarrassing question about who benefits from impoverishing processes. Instead they objectify and stigmatise the poor person - blame the victim. Writing about poverty, Jones and Novak say "Poverty is a corrosive which acts not only through the effects of malnutrition and unhealthy living and working conditions, but also through those social relationships which depict poor as worthless. Surviving poverty is thus not only a matter of trying to balance an inadequate budget. It is also having to deal with the social and psychological stress, with insecurity, social isolation and the often thinly disguised contempt of the more powerful." (Jones, D and Novak, 1999. pp 29,30).

SEEDS OF SOLUTIONS

Faced with these monstrous forces ordinary people have not remained mute. In small yet significant ways they continue to engage and intervene with these systems as collaborators, as resisters and as dissidents etc. However, very few such interventions to address the widening resource gap and deteriorating human condition have transcended personal and local contexts to initiate systemic change. On the face of it, the exploitative forces seem to gain upper hand.

However, in complex systems, the seeds of the solution lie embedded in the same context that created the problem. In keeping with this fact, there have also been simultaneously emergent processes of creative, new ways of engagement at many levels: the individual, the local and the global.

People continue to make meaning of their existence and restore their own purpose and dignity. They resist the stripping of their humanity and their reduction as either machines or raw bodies. They seek justice for the deprivations and damage that they have undergone, so that these violations do not continue. They relate with each other, and evolve ways to imaginatively express their humanity to other significant people that they select. They seek self-validation through this relatedness, and simultaneously express concern for collective living. Even when crafted in silence and alienation, their efforts to reclaim their humanity are loud and clear; and there are a million remarkable testimonies to human creativity and capacity in their daily existence. In this struggle, if large numbers of people who have been impoverished have not taken to the same unethical and violent means that they are subjected to, it is because of this desire, intent and effort.

While many of these strategies are of immense personal significance, such emergent processes rarely receive recognition, nurturance and support. Hence not all of these actions transcend personal courage into structural transformation. Hence their self-determination remains limited. To enable this self-determination, people have to be empowered to act as critical agents who assert their individual rights while holding the governance of their institutions accountable for the collective well-being. For this, they must be willing to be subject to self-regulation, a process of personal determination of values within the context of well-being of others (Pollis, 1992; Baxi, 2003).

RECLAIMING THE GLOBAL CITIZEN

Till now for most part, the notion of the 'global citizen' has been mediated by a select few global elite, through a series of boundaries and rules, over which the exploited and the excluded have little decision-making authority. Economic globalisation forces have also unleashed a bewildering array of institutions and alliances across local and global boundaries. For most part, these institutions have widened the gap between the rich and the poor.

However, the notion of the global citizen has also come to mean more and more, the increasing consciousness of inter-relatedness between human cultures in real time spanning the world. This sharing of values, symbols and perspectives has been particularly instrumental in challenging localised, exploitative relations within people's institutions [for instance, the global feminist and environment conservation movements, the universal human rights framework]. The rapid shifts in alliances and formations at many levels are also forcing more and more people's institutions to find purpose and relevance for their existence.

The nature of the global citizen will be determined by how the local and global meet. If the exchange between the two is on the basis of respect, dignity and equity, and balances individual self-determination with collective well-being; human existence can be transformed radically for the better.

Revisiting Intent, Purpose and Standards: Responsible self-determination and accountable pubic governance are the fulcrums around which processes that impoverish people can be transformed. Increasingly, human self-determination is seen as integrally connected with entitlement to human rights [economic, social, cultural and political] and dignity of all people; particularly those who have been systemically exploited, excluded or impoverished. It is based on the inalienable, universal human rights standards; integral to being human and innate to every person.

Accepting that most people in the planet are not able to exercise their human rights, necessitates personal and collective reflection: re-examination of intent, purpose and standards. To be fruitful, this re-examination must be grounded in human ethics, be rigorous and transparent rather than tokenistic or opportunistic, with genuine intent to identify personal and systemic factors that impoverish people. It has to forefront issues of personal and collective accountability. People, particularly the resourceful population, will have to transform their behaviour, while simultaneously seeking methods to increase and support the agency of people that have been affected (Falk, 2000).

Such re-examination cannot be nostalgic, glorifying the past; or indifferent and apathetic to the human condition. This scrutiny need not be violent or guilt-ridden; and instead can be creative and celebratory, finding ways to restore relevance without stripping people of perspective and dignity.

For example, the 'Where do You Keep Your Racism' Campaign by the Diálogos Contra o Racismo (Dialogues Against Racism) group is one such innovative strategy used by the black movement in Brazil aimed to start discussions about thoughts, habits and attitudes that encode racism and reveal the diverse nature of racist expressions and re-examine them; so as to surface unconsciously held racist positions. The Dialogue Against Racism is a platform of over 40 civil-society organisations, most of which do not belong to the black movement. The initiative was to visibilise racial prejudice, particularly to those who do not suffer its effects, so that racism as an issue becomes a concern not just of black people but the entire society.

Critical Citizen's Collectives: Critical, transparent and accountable governance systems are essential, benchmarked against universal human rights; to actualise the idea of a critical, global citizen. For this, people's institutions must function in the 'public sphere' as critical opinion-making bodies as characterised by Habermass (1981)[iii]. In his understanding of these critical citizen's collectives, reference is not made only of their participation in electoral politics. This is still an ongoing endeavour, with democracy still to mature. What it instead refers to is the active debate and action in the public sphere, least controlled by sentiments and bonded by the desire to evolve public opinion from below.

In the current scenario, there have been some collectives that have played this critical role. Many of these make decisions on egalitarian principles. They undertake honest, courageous, self-correcting reflection on their reality. They integrate the interrelatedness fostered by traditional institutions; and fraternity promoted by modern institutions. Hence they have been able to transcend their individual purpose to determine the public sphere [caste, gender, ethnicity, and race] to enable human well-being. Often these collective have emerged spontaneously, are reflective and creative, rather than target-driven and instrumental.

These collectives have been embedded in different contexts to varying degrees creating affirmative institutions: the state with its welfare function; the development sector with its focus on people's participation; people's movements with their focus on human rights and empowerment; voluntary social organisations with concern for the well-being of humanity; traditional institutions of relatedness, nurturance and equity, as well as respect for their environment and nature; modern institutions' emphasis on the spirit of fraternity, particularly among strangers; peer networks that emphasise inclusion in new ways and egalitarian decision-making; and civil society groups demanding accountability from state and market as citizens and consumers.

Where such affirmative institutions and nascent processes exist, they do so in spite of the norm. One reason for this is that they are emergent, filled with subjective and diverse stories of personal symbols and transformations. The dominant western, rational approach with its models of cause and effect remain ill-equipped to understand or value these diverse perspectives and is threatened by them. Hence these processes tend to be regarded with suspicion, and are ignored or poorly supported. If enabled and supported these affirmative acts hold within them the real potential of rejuvenating human well-being.

RESTORATION OF PEOPLE'S INSTITUTIONS

In the new context of economic globalisation, people's institutions (family, State, etc.) are being forced to revisit their purpose in their search for continued relevance. This provides an opportunity to rejuvenate traditional institutions and humanise modern ones.

Rejuvenation of Traditional Institutions: The rejuvenation of people's institutions has to be on several levels – family, community, nation, and globe. There are many proximal traditional institutions in the lives of the exploited and the impoverished that are badly wounded, discredited and destroyed currently. Old women gathering, caste groups, youth gatherings, friendship networks, indigenous kin-based groups in tribal belts, religious groups, women's networks, livelihood sects are few such instances that hold deep potential for individual and societal transformation.

These institutions must be examined for their relevance in the current scenario, by revisiting their intent, purpose and values through the human rights framework. They must also transform inherent hierarchical, discriminatory and exploitative tendencies [such as gender, caste, race; as well as impoverishment and exclusion]; that are embodied in their members. This transformation requires sensitive and patient iterative engagement to repair damage, regain trust, build métis and restore morale.

The wisdom of traditional institutions must be revalidated and reaccredited. The pride in their functioning must also be restored, while simultaneously releasing them from self serving and opportunistic positions. In this rejuvenation, form and function must be given equal importance; so that there is no nostalgic attachment of old and sometimes irrelevant forms; with the focus remaining on the rejuvenation of their original functions of inter-dependence, nurturance and relatedness.

Humanising Modern Institutions: Modern institutions have come under increasing scrutiny (Kothari, 1988) in current times, particularly around issues related to people's participation in governance. This along with the demands of economic globalisation has forced these institutions to seek their relevance and revisit their purpose.

There is increasing recognition that modern institutions are rapidly becoming unaccountable to the people and civil society who belong to them. Often, their development agendas are more geared towards profit for a few, rather than collective human well-being. It is also recognised that to remain relevant to their members, these institutions must humanise their perspectives; acknowledge that complex human systems cannot be reduced to mechanised systems alone. As a result, there is the increasing focus on people's participation and decision-making; and dialogue and partnerships across sectors.

The focus on people's participation has engineered a wide array of community institutions that have often been self-organising [such as savings and credit groups, people's co-operatives]. When these groups address issues of discrimination, they have aided the transformation from traditional hierarchical exploitative structures to horizontal networks of peers or interest groups that share knowledge and resources for common purpose.

For instance, increasingly, there is recognition that cash economies dehumanizes people and decreases community solidarity. This recognition has led to the re-personalisation of money through community currency initiatives across the world. To counter the loss of relatedness and the insecurity of working in an international market that undervalue local produce, local communities in Thailand organized themselves into an alternate, local economy creating a community currency called Bia Kud Chum. The Bia is just one example amongst several other nascent community currency efforts across the world: for instance, in Japan, LETS (Local Exchange Trading Systems) and HOURS; in Mexico, the Tlaloc mutual credit system.

The Bia (local currency) is equivalent to the Thai Baht; and cannot be used outside its network of groups and communities. This very insularity of the currency ensures that local resources remain within communities and ensures their self sufficiency. This effort emerged from a larger trend of community based initiatives and "self sufficiency groups" around several livelihood activities: a rice mill supporting chemical free rice production, cooperative shops, and women's groups producing soya milk, herbal shampoo and dishwashing liquid. This currency has been condemned by national financial bodies that see such efforts as a threat to their own existence and functioning. As a result, communities in five villages have been accused of breaking the law.

Reformulating the Nation-State: Given that that the nation state has actively partnered in economic globalization process, its governance functions are now being determined increasingly by global, private capital forces; often at the cost of its welfare functions. When confronted with complex challenges, the state has been indifferent to most people's experiences concerns or incapable of responding to them, resulting in growing societal discontent, as well as inequity and injustice.

The State even while largely failing on its social welfare function, yet came into being mostly with promises of democratic equality and human rights. In these aspirations, it reflected the collective aspirations of their citizens.

Observing that the state continues to deeply concern its citizens, John Harris (2002) states "the state in India might indeed be rotten, but it is not accurate to say that ordinary men and women have lost faith entirely in the idea of the state" (page 2-3). Even others who are severely critical of the state agree that the state is still a critical mobilizing agency (Dipankar Gupta, 2002) and is yet to exhaust its possibilities for releasing the poor from poverty.

To fulfil its promise, the democratic nation-state has to base all its actions on the realisation of universal human rights and entitlements. It must move beyond its economic agendas to a genuine concern to people's well-being and dignity. It must accord respect to people's intelligence and self-determination; and must renew its pact with its citizenry to realise their individual and collective aspiration and well-being. For this, it must be committed to people's participation and decision-making. Its public governance must remain pro-people (for instance, pro-poor). In particular, people who have been exploited or excluded must be included in public governance: by honouring their human rights; by reviving their institutions; by ensuring enabling their self-determination; by supporting them conserve their environments and their valuing their métis; and by restoring respect and faith in their own intent, purpose and values. Finally, it must establish transparent government practices to continue remaining accountable to its citizenry.

In recent times, there has been increasing questioning of the state's role, authority and accountability, particularly by people's movements and critical, citizen's groups across the world. As a result, people who have been exploited or excluded are directly beginning to hold the State accountable for its actions on several standards.

The rapid global-level changes in the last few decades years have forced the state itself to reinvent its relevance in ways not fully understood. The state's response to this call for reformulation has been mixed; though largely discouraging, not entirely without its positive elements.

For instance, even as the welfare state has devolved its responsibilities (creation of user fees for instance for basic services such as education and health), it has also engaged in decentralisation processes to local governance institutions. The 73rd and 74th amendments of the Indian constitution are two such examples.

In other instances, the state urged by civil society and enlightened leadership have shown concern for their citizens. In India, the introduction of the NREGA (National Rural Employment Guarantee Act) in August 2005 is a landmark social security policy This differs from other past employment guarantee schemes in three important ways: guaranteeing employment could not be terminated by administrative decree; employment would not be restricted to applicants holding Below Poverty Line cards; and the schemes would be implemented through local governance bodies. These progressive measures were introduced in spite of considerable internal opposition from various government bodies, because of several reasons: national movements to end hunger, the electoral imperative to introduce pro-poor public policy in a country where more than half the population is poor, and sensitive and intelligent political leadership aware of the reasons and consequences of failure.

In Brazil, the re-democratisation efforts and the constitution reformulation in 1988 propelled by demands of people's movement in the country set forth measures to ensure people's participation in public policy as well as recognised the role of civil society in the political systems resulting it being called the 'citizen constitution'.

The role of collegiate institutions of Public Policy Councils to actively determine public policy was a revolution in the country's governance where public policy decisions were not restricted to just the State Executive but also extended to civic society representatives. They have already been significant in determining national policy regarding health, and social work policies for children and adolescents.

Between 2003 and 2006, about 40 national conferences attended by over two million people (union members, NGOs, social movements, professional and corporate associations, churches, etc.) and representatives of municipal, state, and federal agencies. In the national phase of these conferences alone, about 5,000 public deliberations were held. The inputs from these deliberations were incorporated into different sectoral public policies (Institute for Applied Economic Research 2007, p. 20). In this instance, conferences as a medium of people's participation have enabled people's contribution in determining public policies.

Again, in many instances, the nation-state is also recognising the importance of representation of traditionally exploited and excluded people in decision-making through its reservation policies. For instance, during the administration of President Lula in Brazil, more black men and women were included in high-ranking positions; where previously it was markedly absent. Again the reservation for women in governance systems in India, while largely being symbolic, also has positively impacted people's perspectives about gender in some instances.

Holding Corporates Responsible: Current global markets have forced individuals to work across diverse contexts, in time. space, values and culture. In this scenario, the very intent and nature of work has undergone massive transformations. This has fundamentally challenged the linear, instrumental understanding of human work; and necessitated institutions to reflect on working in complex systems. This is most apparent in the increasing emphasis on human resource management and on corporate social responsibility. Both these trends hold seeds for future change transforming negative impacts into positive ones on human well-being.

One consequence of the shift in understanding of work and efficiency is the increasing relevance of human resource development, both as a science and practice. This relevance has been further increased by the burgeoning service industry. In some instances, this shift in perspective has created alternate spaces of individual and collective reflection, focused on personal and organisational development, and leadership. Even as many of these reflections challenge existing discrimination, their main purpose remains generation of individual profit. Only a few of these reflections transcend this intent into structural transformation based on human rights values.

Called to be accountable by civil society groups, corporates are beginning to contend with social and ecological consequences of their singular focus on profits. As part of this, they are beginning to not just invest more resources in development aid, they are also creating communities of committed professionals and workers who are willing to volunteer their services for this. However, the intent behind such interventions is still not completely transparent; and often does not transform discriminatory practices within the institution. It must also be acknowledged that even their best of intentions to contribute to development and welfare in the name of Corporate Social Responsibility, have been inadequate even in redressing the damages their own profit-seeking activities have caused.

SUPPORT OF EMERGENT INSTITUTIONS AND PROCESSES

In addition to restoration of current people institutions, new forms of organising and formulations that are affirmative have to be supported. Three emergent people's institutions and processes are critical.

Movements and Campaigns: People's movements and campaigns have played an integral role in causing systemic change for human well-being in current times. Some of these movements and collectives have shown tremendous unconditional support for the disempowered. Hence, in many instances, they have created institutions that emphasise equitable decision-making and empowerment; restoring people's sense of control over their lives. This role rests as much as on their taking unequivocal stances against injustice and violation; as their willingness to take responsibility for and reflect on their experiences, and correct themselves.

Movements are organized around universal human rights values of dignity, equity, autonomy, community sovereignty, conservation, and justice. Many of these processes have been led by individuals who have themselves been exploited or excluded. Since they are often immersed in individual and localized experience, and devote considerable effort to reflect on justice and equity, they address some systemic reasons that create discrimination. Since they place importance on self-expression, particularly by those who have been marginalised and silenced, they empower self-determination. They also recognize that interventions needed for human well-being cannot just be individualistic, but must be collectivist.

However, in their emphasis on collective change, they often neglect to address issues related to individual meaning-making and self-actualisation. These institutions are still embedded in the dominant western, scientific paradigms and suffer from the same maladies of a monocular rationalistic perspective. They fall into the trap that most modern institutions find themselves in: reduction of human experience, denying both the emotional and the reflective; and focusing inordinately on the material; fragmenting their perspectives and rendering them reactive. Further their work is often at the edge of people's survival. The urgency imparted by the nature of this work does not permit time for personal reflection; aggravating their reactivity.

There are some shifts that are occurring in recent times in the purpose and intent of these people's movements, as a result of peer sharing across the globe. One is a shift from concerns of only distribution of material resources, to concerns of identity and dignified human self-determination. Thus, even while recognizing the importance of material well-being, people's movements have begun to reflect on other aspects of the human experience. Second, since movements consider human collectivism as a foundation value of their work, social movements work in an inter-related manner, forming the basis of global movements – the labour movement, the women's movement, the peace movement, the secular movement, environment movement – complex layers that intersect each other. In the success of this inter-related work, their own grounding in local realities plays an important role.

The impact of social movements is as yet unclear. When movements have been able to balance individual and collective demands, they have resulted in significant transformation. One example is the effort on the part of the women's movement to examine gender role constructs, by reflecting on both individual and collective experience.

Open Source Knowledge Banks: In the last few decades, there have been radical transformations on how people across vast geographical differences know and relate with each other because of advances in digital information technology. Information is now more readily available and is more prone to accumulation and dispersal than ever before. One significant outcome of this is the World Wide Web. With the intent to remain autonomous, and following values of open access, the internet has offered unprecedented access to open source knowledge repositories. Further it makes this information available across geographical boundaries, and cultures. More and more people are beginning to take part in this endeavour and grapple with the values underpinning the formation of open source knowledge repositories and their networks of transaction.

Peer-Sharing and Communities of Interest: One outcome of the transformation in global knowledge sharing is the strengthening of diverse voices with varying intent and perspectives in the public domain; with more and people structurally exploited or excluded being able to articulate their reality. Attempts to control and homogenise these voices are becoming difficult.

There have also been unprecedented shifts in peer sharing across vast geographical distances, cosmologies and in real time. These have resulted in autonomous, local and diverse forms of organising. Already across the globe, communities of interest [rather than just geographical proximal communities] are in communication with each other, often to serve a common purpose. These communities often structure themselves along the lines of the horizontal network structure of the web that serve as the platform of their exchange. This horizontal sharing has altered traditional hierarchical and exclusive patterns of sharing knowledge and practice.

Even as it has deepened sharing within common interest areas, it also created inter-dependent relations with those from different contexts and perspectives. This has led to the emergency of new forms of communities based on inter-disciplinary interests that offer solutions in complex systems. These new communities form networks that span the globe, while remaining rooted in their local contexts. This has enabled the led to the re-knitting of individual and collective meaning making in new ways. In some instances, these citizens' fora have become locations of spontaneous transformative collective action that challenged exploitation and exclusion and restructured the public sphere.

Even as we celebrate these, we deeply recognise its limited reach, as these peer-sharing mechanisms and open source knowledge banks depend on certain degree of apprenticeship in using them effectively and on hardware, whose penetration is not widespread. Vast majority of the poor still remain outside the ambit of digital technologies. In this context it would do well to remember Castells (2000) caution about placing too much faith on information networks, because it is, "characterised by double movement: on the one hand valuable segments of territories and people are linked in the global networks of value making and wealth appropriation. On the other hand, everything, and everyone, which does not have value, according to what is valued in the networks, or ceases to have value, is switched off the networks and ultimately discarded". (p.134)

Yet, this limitation or caution does not diminish the optimism we have about its potential for the positive transformative impact.

IN CONCLUSION

The human condition is deteriorating rapidly for many people because of the fragmentation of their traditional institutions, the indifference of the modern ones to human well-being, the destruction of nature and commons, and the failure of the nation state in its governance functions. As a result, more and more people are being impoverished and rendered dispensable, left to fend for their survival against insurmountable odds.

The urgency and scale with which the poor are being eradicated requires us to respond urgently. This action cannot be reactive and fragmented. Instead, this action must be holistic, and address systemic root causes of exploitation and exclusion. It must acknowledge the complex and intelligent nature of human and natural systems, their emergence and inter-relatedness. It must be committed to enabling an honest appraisal of the self and the context, revisiting intent, purpose and ethical standards. These standards have to be clear and steadfast. Guided by these ethical standards, action must aim to empower people and affirm their self-determination so as to enable their participation in public governance.

Even though the challenge faced seems insurmountable, in complex systems, solutions to current problems also lie embedded in this same system. There are several seeds of action that are emerging currently: restoration of current institutions, by rejuvenating traditional ones and humanising modern ones; formation of global and local collectivities, particularly people's movements in redressing justice and equity issues, and newly emergent peer networking and open source knowledge repositories based on horizontal networks rather than hierarchical structures. These potential systemic solutions are now being recognised and articulated.

To meet the challenge posed by impoverishing processes, there has to be a collective shift in a critical mass of people about the purpose of their institutions; when people are no longer evoked to act for limited self-gain, but also proactively act to critically determine public governance. Such critical citizen collectives may well be the pivot around which the cycle of poverty turns.

End notes:

[i] Mills, page 4

[ii] Philip Steinberg's 2001 book *The Social Construction of the Ocean*

[iii] Mostly for modern institutions, but can also be extrapolated to traditional and other forms of people's organising; Habermass, J. 1981, *The Colonisation of Public Sphere*, Polity Press, London.

X

The Swing of the Pendulum: Community care to collective care

The plea for de-institutionalisation and community care for the dependent population_[1] is based on the deep frustration with and fair degree of suspicion about the horrific conditions in the institutional and residential care centres. It is also predicated upon the clinical and sociological evidences that suggest that these dependent populations such as old age people, disabled and mentally ill feel cared and could regain the strength of their morale in family and community contexts rather than in the institutional and residential care centres. The concern for the dependent people and the conviction with which the plea is aired can never be mistaken, or exaggerated.

The precedents

Indeed, the argument in favour of community care had been raised in the western world in the sixties itself. Particularly in Great Britain, such demands for de-institutionalisation were advocated, very curiously, by all the stakeholders in the care for dependent population, namely, the political leaders, the professionals and voluntary organizations. The next few years saw the enthusiastic implementation of the idea of community care in Britain and also in the USA. The concrete forms of such programmes were, foster homes, hostels, halfway houses, and family care. The longer-than-a-decade experiments with community care had brought to surface many of the strengths and, more importantly, numerous problems. At one point the negative consequences of these efforts became so acutely striking that the Select Committee was asked to look into it. The Select Committee thus highlighted many of the problems associated with community care and de-institutionalisation efforts. We will see some of the salient points of the Select Committee Reports in a while, but before that a quick look at other trends that contributed to the emerging disenchantment with community care.

<u>The challenges</u>

Principally the disparaging attack on community care models came from feminist quarters. This is despite their sharing the frustration with institutional and residential care. Yet their enthusiasm for alternative solutions did not include community care in the sense in which it was advocated. In that sense they stood on the same platform erected by the collectivist lobby. They were indeed arguing for a collective responsibility of which community responsibility was a part. In matters of practice they advocated collectivist living style as a solution to the problems of institutional care.

Another trend that came to influence the critics of community care was that which was advocated by the collectivists themselves. The unbearably rugged individualism and familialism (particularly nuclear family ideals) that characterised the discourses of community care were stoutly opposed by the collectivists. The exact contents of their contestations will be elaborated below.

<u>The precipitation</u>

The arrival of a social policy is invariably expressive of the moral climate in which it is enunciated. Similarly when the first attempts were made in offering institutional care to the dependent population, it smacked of patronism and deep productivist bias. The industrial culture that was establishing itself stridently in Europe divided the entire population into two categories – the ones who could contribute to production thorough their labor and the other who could not, due to their impairments of mind and body. The latter were labeled as the dependent population. Simultaneously any one who could do labour (the able bodied) but uninvolved in production was severely punished and put in workhouses. The group of dependent population was declared to be deserving of care and support out of the excess wealth now made possible by the industrial revolution. The process of separation of the dependent population from the rest happened systematically and carefully with all the good intentions going behind it. The dependent population was brought under the custody of institutional care so as to enable the productive population to focus on making positive contribution to industrial production. The assistance of the medical establishment in assisting in the exercise of classification and overseeing of the dependent population has never been more elaborately documented. But there were repeated accusations about the manner in which these institutions and theirs medical gatekeepers went about pathologising the inmates. Soon the dehumanising nature of these institutions and the manner in which they perpetuated the inmates' dependency rather than releasing them from the custodialisation were brought to public notice.

The increasing disappointment and disillusionment with the institutional care led its opponents to demand community care as the best way to provide better quality of life to the dependent population. Planners, professionals and voluntary workers gleefully seized upon this idea. This again is symptomatic of the time in which it was envisaged. The compulsion to cut the cost and lessen the burden of the middle class tax payer were some of the reasons why the planners and the state representatives were very enthusiastic about it. The medical professionals and other technocrats were excited about the possibility of privatised health care that could proliferate, as the loosening of the hold of the state welfarist ideals has thrown the population out in the open to handle the harsh reality of the public sphere on their own. The social work professionals were arguing for rehumanising the care itself. Though the rehumanisation of the public sphere was the undergirding ambition behind community care initiatives, the vested interests of the politicians and medical professionals were overriding these concerns.

While the community care practices were coming under increasing scrutiny by various groups including feminists and collectivists, the problems faced both by the cared and carers in a variety of community settings were unignorably evident even for the votaries of the community care models. Many of those who were de-institutionalised were slipping into intensely aggravated conditions, such as homelsessness, begging, destitution and worsened mental illness. The carers themselves complained of stress, irritability, and frustration in caring for the dependents. This led to many modified practices. Delayed discharge of the patients and inmates so as to identify better carers, and turning the previously custodial institutions into "guesthouses" where the returning inmates would be regarded as "guests" till they are put back into community care were to name a few.

The culmination of the discontent with community care model was the confessional statement from the British government itself that community care model was a failure. Assuaging such pessimism and resignation, the Select Committee, which was inquiring into mental health rehabilitation measures, made the following observations in 1980,

There have been undeniable failures in service since the policy of care in the community was first launched. But we feel that it is both misleading and unhelpful to state that the policy of care in the community has failed, *as the Government has done on a number of occasions* (emphasis added). We urge the Government to make clear in the language it uses (as indeed it has already done in the policies it has embraced), that care in the community is a positive policy and one which it supports (paragraph 39).

The response of the government was, though mindful of the limitations of community care, largely in favour of community care. It says:

The Government has never given any indication that it does not support the provision of effective community mental health services. But we would have been failing in our duty if we had not made clear our view that, in practice, a number of people were let down, sometimes with tragic results, by the piecemeal way in which the policy of community care was implemented and by the lack of suitable support services. With the benefit of hindsight we can say that the initial plans for introducing community care were over-optimistic and did not anticipate a range of problems which have contributed to failures in implementation (emphasis added). The key issue, however, is to learn the lessons from these past failures and to take steps to rectify them. We have done much in the last three years to demonstrate our commitment to providing a comprehensive and effective range of modern community and in-patient services, which are based upon evidence of effectiveness. The debate is no longer about institutionalisation versus community care but about how to assure provision of a range of services which services users and carers have told us they want and need.

Thus, the present model of community care has gone through many reviews and restructuring as it was responding to various criticisms and currents of opinion. What has evolved in the present context of caring for the dependency is a model that has the elements of community and collectivist care rolled into one. Even if that is not what has come to obtain in reality, that is what is aspired. As the Select Committee recommendations suggest:

It is clear from the evidence we received that the environment of the traditional hospital is not the best environment for helping individuals in crisis: people suffering acute phases of mental illness may need a "safe haven" away from their own homes, and sometimes secure surroundings, but this need not be in an institutional building. Indeed, the use of such buildings appears to be based on necessity rather than on any belief that they are the best or only way of providing care to individuals in distress.

We recognise the need to balance domesticity, good quality care and security (emphasis added) which is emphasised in the Royal College of Psychiatrists' report 'Not just Bricks and Mortar'. However, we do believe that further research on how these aims can best be achieved would be very valuable. We therefore urge the Department to fund pilot schemes following the *"core and cluster" model* (emphasis added) described by Professor Rowden and Dr. Moodley, so that their effectiveness can be rigorously evaluated. If such pilot schemes are successful, we recommend that the Department commit itself to providing the capital expenditure necessary to expand them swiftly (paragraph 101).

However such an integrated model did not always address the concerns raised by the feminists and collectivists, and considering them in detail will help us in India to evolve a more sensitive caregiving model for the dependent population of various kinds including mentally ill persons.

Feminist Concerns

The rush for community-based care for the dependent population had taken the dependent populations away from the custody of the institutional care to small-scale homes, hostels and halfway houses etc. But in practice the community care model hardly turned out be really a community responsibility. Eventually, the care of the dependent population was vested in the shoulders of the women, if not in the form of mothers, daughters, sisters and wives, at least in the form of carers. Particularly this singular contribution from the womenfolk, apart from confirming the already solidified stereotype of women-as-cares, always goes unpaid. Expressing the concern that all these efforts to return the caregiving functions to the community has only entailed a situation in which the burden on the family, and exclusively women in it, has become heavier. Gillan Dalley says

Despite the growing burden [on the immediate family] there is no evidence of any involvement by the wider community – friends, neighbours, volunteers and even extended family members – in providing any one of the care which is needed from day-to-day. Instead the burden of care falls on the young person's mother or results in marked financial, physical and emotional costs (See, Gillan Dalley, *Ideology of Caring*, MacMillan, London, 1988).

'Care for' and 'care about' functions

This burdening of the women is mostly the result of the uncritical acceptance of the ideologically constructed notions of motherhood and even womanhood. As Dalley makes it abundantly clear, the conflation of 'caring for' functions with 'caring about' functions has spelt disaster for women in all circumstances and heaped more burdens on women. It is instructive that we consider the differences between these two acts to see as to how it burdens women on the one hand and also as to how the collective care that we wish to ensure for the dependent population can be organized better.

Actually the act of 'caring for' somebody is to attend to the physical and psychic needs of the individuals who cannot achieve them on their own, whereas 'caring about' is all about understanding and responding to the emotions of the concerned persons. A mother who 'cares about' her daughter very deeply still may employ some one to 'care for' her or even enroll her in the best of the places where she is sure that her daughter will be 'cared for' better. But in reality it is not. She cannot do it without running the risk of being labeled as a bad mother, particularly in those circumstances in which the said child or children were physically disabled and mentally ill. The traditional compulsions are such that the very person who 'cares about' the dependent person is also supposed to 'care for' her/him. Invariably the woman who 'cares about' ends up 'caring for' the dependent person just to appear as a complete woman. It is exactly because of this conflation between the 'care for' and 'care about' functions that women are forced to engage with the care of the dependent, even in community care situations. In many of the lifehistories that we have collected of dependent people we have found this overburdening of women wherever it has been decided to retain the dependent person at home. May be in those rare cases we would have men performing these functions. But they are exceptions rather than rules.

On the contrary, the case of men is different. They can 'care about' a person, say his daughter, yet he can get away without personally 'caring for' the child. This is because he is just expected to be responsible for ensuring the 'care for' functions to his child by employing a wet nurse or some assistant.

Therefore when moving from institutional care to alternative ways of caring it is very important that we keep these distinctions in mind and do not end up overburdening the women. And precisely these differences should also help us to view the institutional care in more reasonable light. It is in the nature of the institution-centred care that they can never substitute the 'caring about' functions offered by a range of people who are proximate to the dependent persons. At best these institutions could do the 'caring for' functions, if they are organized effectively.

Much of our pessimism for institutional and residential care is born of our collapsing the differences between the two modes of caring – 'caring for' and 'caring about'. And equally much of our disillusionment with community care is again the outcome of the same collapsing. Expecting the institution-centred care to perform the 'caring about' functions is as unreasonable as expecting the community-centred care (which is basically women-centred care) to offer the 'care for' functions. Perhaps if we redefine our expectations and organise the caregiving structures in such a manner that the 'caring about' person could have a space in the 'caring for' institutions and vice versa then a solution may emerge.

But ideally the feminist response is not favour of a compromise between these two. They indeed argue for a model, which demands a collective responsibility from various actors and agencies among which what could be the responsibility of the community (as provider of the 'caring about' functions) and institutional setups (as provider of the 'caring for' functions) are just two instances. They call for holding several other stakeholders in the welfare of the dependent population responsible, including the state apparatus, the medical establishment, social work professionals and neighbourhoods and friendship networks etc. Presumably something closer to these sentiments are echoed by the Select Committee when it made the Recommendation Y, though this does not predicate itself upon the collectivist school of thought. It reads as follows:

It is clear to us that a far more "joined-up" response is necessary from statutory agencies if users of mental health services are to be properly supported in the community. We do not believe it is acceptable or realistic to expect vulnerable individuals to deal with complex systems without support, especially where it is clear that these systems are ill equipped to deal with fluctuating illness. *We would encourage the Department to give particular attention to the idea of a dedicated worker, who would be responsible for liaising between the various statutory agencies and ensuring that users of mental health services, living in the community, have access to the benefits and other services to which they are entitled.* (emphasis added)

All the same, the call for collective responsibility or collective care is just only one important aspects of the collectivist response. There is another important and crucial aspect of the collectivist response that has a lot to do with collective living itself. The clarity might arrive if we dwell upon the precise arguments of the collectivist response.

Collectivist response

Collectivists strongly rally themselves against the community caregiving models that privilege and idealise family as the one and only provider of care and insurance against rootlessness and insecurity. As argued above, idealisation of the family particularly in caring the dependent people unduly burdens the women in it. On the other count also it is unacceptable. Because locating the careability to the dependent only in the family is tantamount to freeing many other actors and agencies from assuming such crucial responsibilities which they ought to do for caring the dependent persons. And in a true social-psychological sense confining the dependent persons to the boundaries of the family (which is what ultimately happens in the name of community care), sharply undermines and curtails their social skills, as they have narrow possibilities for associational life inside the families. Thus collectivist, in a true collectivist spirit, would place high premium on the associational life as the wellspring of human freedom and dignity.

Association as the source of freedom

The crude individualist notions define freedom as the ability of and the condition for an individual to avoid and ward off the usurpers of his/her liberty (in other words *avoidance of evil*), wherein such abilities and conditions are *achieved* by the individual. But the collectivist traces individual freedom[2] to the ability of and condition for an individual to *do good* to other in the company of others, wherein such abilities and conditions themselves are *created* by others including the self. These, by extension, would mean that the free, dignified and well-cared life for the dependent is not the responsibility of the concerned individual or his family alone, it is rather the responsibility of the larger set of social actors and structures with which the individual associates and *ought to associate*. The fact that they *ought to associate* should behoove us to create such conditions in which the dependent individuals could lead a life in association with people like her/him, people of her/his choice and in the midst of people and structures clearly mindful of their responsibilities.

Alternatives

In keeping with the above sentiments, some of the alternatives suggested by the collectivists are hospitals turned into communes in which larger decisions and charge for the every day activities are taken by the dependent population themselves, but aided and assisted by the non-judgemental, clearly pro-dependent-persons experts and professionals (we shall call them 'hinge groups'). In these communes the parents and foster parents could share the living space with their dependent relatives if both party mutually desire so. In all these situations any one who volunteers to spend their days with the dependent population, even if they are their parents and immediate relatives, should be compensated financially by paying an allowance. This way even the otherwise unpaid women in community care situations are rewarded economically. The state responsibilities to these communes are same, if not more, as what obtained in the previous situations. Highly organised volunteer programmes could ensure that more than known-only people come to live with the dependent populations.

We could create even a dependent population-run and -managed villages and farms. In Europe we have such villages (in India we can recall Asha Gram), run by aged people duly assisted by non-old population. For mentally ill people too such grams or villages could be visualised. These villages could be managed by the discharged persons, as well as by the ones who evince self-control and other signs of coming to terms with reality around them, again appropriately *assisted* and *aided* by professionals of all hues and shades.

Whatever may be the alternative forms we envisage they should foster the following five cardinal principles for ensuring a humane care. They are:

- The dependent person has the right and ability to be responsible for her/his own life and this must be honoured and strengthened. It is not to argue for total independence but to have the choice to decide which kind and type of dependency they wish to rely upon. This applies both to the cared and carer.

- The care offered should be responsive to the needs and inclinations of the cared. The care given should be flexible and movement between different forms of care must be possible when appropriate.

- Maximal opportunity to form as wide and varied a range of personal relationship as the individual might wish.

- Maximal opportunity to develop skills and talents in any way that the individual chooses.

- Dependent people should be economically secure. Payment of allowance to the cared and carer is one such strategy.

Caveats in lieu of Conclusion

We would conclude this paper by introducing few caveats.

If I have been very critical of community care policies, it is not because I do not see the importance of 'caring for' and 'caring about' or of the necessity of enabling disabled and chronologically-dependent to live normalised and ordinary lives. Nor is it to deny that people want to be 'cared for' in familiar surroundings and to be 'cared about' by people about whom they themselves care. It is just I am concerned that the care given to them happens in an environment and condition where there is an assurance and active demonstration of collective responsibility, partaken of by every stakeholder.

Secondly, we must also remember that all is not terrible with institutional care. It should continue to be available (only after purging it of its self-aggrandizing and dehumanising elements) to those who choose to seek such care. The fundamental assumption that community-based forms of care are appropriate to all categories of dependency should be as rigorously questioned as the assumption that all forms of institutional and residential care are unacceptable. There are many people who need the safety and security of the institutional care both in the sense of haven and refuge, away from the stresses and rigour of the outside world. Expecting the dependent population to fight against the stresses and rigour arising out of the heartlessness of the non-disabled people all by themselves with the assistance only of their family members is unjust.

Thirdly, the precedents that are observable in other countries caution us to be mindful of replicating some of the problem situations in India too. When writing about the community care models in the context of social policy in Britain, Jones writes, "What has followed community care initiatives in Britain is increasing surveillance, assessment and evaluation of state on family's performance. As the responsibilities for care had been vested in community, the continued demonstration of delinquency and nuisance is punished severely by the state. However this time the punishment is given to the parents and carers through such orders as Parenting order, Child safety orders and Crime and Disorder Act". The shifting of responsibilities from the state to community still only enhances the disciplinary power of the state only.

And finally we must also rethink whether the traditional Indian society was specifically characterised by community care ideals or collective care ideals. I am inclined to thinking that the remnants of the various caregiving models of the past that still stay with us in whatever shapes, as religion-centred asylums etc., seem to be collectivist models gone fractured and twisted than community care gone wrong. It, however, goes with out saying that our community life always had accepted and accommodated the dependent populations.

End notes:

[1] Dependent population here includes people in old age, disabled, mentally ill.

[2] Collectivists would rather call for egalitarianism than freedom, as the former subsumes the latter.

BIBLIOGRAPHY

Abu-Lughod, J.L (1991), "Going beyond Global Babble" in A.D King (ed.) *Culture, Globalization and the world-system*, MacMillan, London.

Altekar. A. S. (1962), *The Position of Women in Hindu*

Appadurai, Arjun (1986), "Introduction: Commodities and the Politics of Value" in A. Appadurai (edited) *The Social life of things*, Cambridge University Press.

Baldev, Rai Nayar (2000), *Globalization and Nationalism: The Changing Balance In India's Economic Policy 1950-2000*, Sage Publications, New Delhi.

Baulch, B and McCulloch, N. 1998. Being Poor and Becoming Poor: Poverty Status and Poverty Transition in Rural Poor. *IDS Working Paper*: No 79. Brighton, IDS.

Bauman, Zygmant, *The Bauman Reader*, Polity Press, London, 2001

Bauman, Zygmut (1998) *Globalization: The Human Consequences*, Cambridge: Polity Press.

Baxi, U. 2003. *Human Rights*. Oxford University Press. Delhi.

Castells, Manuel, (2000), *The Rise of the Network Society*, Vol1, Oxford, Basil Blackwell.

Castells, Manuel. 2001. *The Internet Galaxy—Reflections on the Internet, Business and Society.* Oxford University Press.

Chamber, R. 1997. *Whose Reality Counts? Putting the First Last.* London. Intermediate Technology.

Chambers, R. 1995. 'Poverty and Livelihoods: Whose Reality Counts?' *IDS Discussion Paper 347.*

Chambers, R. 2001. 'The World Development Report: Concepts, Contents and a Chapter 12', *Journal of International Development*, Vol.13, 299–306.

Chambers, Robert, N.C.Saxena and Tushar Shah. 1989. *To the Hands of the Poor*, Intermediate Technology Publications.

Dalley, Gillan. 1988. *Ideology of Caring*, MacMillan, London

Das, Veena (ed) 1990. Mirrors of Violence. Oxford University Press, New Delhi.

Dreze, J and Sen, A. 1999. 'Public Action and Social Inquality', in Subramaniam and Harris, Barbara (Eds). *Illfare in India*. Sage. New Delhi.

Dreze, Jean 2002. "On Research and Action", in *Economic and Political Weekly*, March 02.

Editorial. 2000. Marginalisation of Tribals. *Economic and Political Weekly*; November 18.

Falk, Richard (2000), *Human Rights Horizon*, Routledge, New York.

George, Vic, 1985. *Ideology of Welfare*, RKP, London

Gerentitz, Z. 2002. *Bauman Reader*, Blackwell, London.

Green, Maria. 2002, *Representing Poverty: Attacking Representations*, Paper presented at Chronic Poverty conference, London.

Gupta, Dipankar. Civil Society and the State: What happened to Citizenship, in Guha, R. and Jonatahn Parry (Eds). *Institutions and Inequalities*. Oxford University Press. Delhi. 2002

Habermass, J. 1981, *The Colonisation of Public Spehere*, Polity Press, London

Hannerz, Ulf (1991), Culture, *Globalisation and the World-System*, MacMillan, London.

Harris, B. 1999. 'On to a Loser: Diability in India', in Subramaniam and Harris, Barbara (Eds). *Illfare in India*. Sage. NewDelhi.

Harris, Barabara. State, Market Collective and Household Action in India's Social Sector in Subramaniam and Harris, Barbara (Eds). 1999. *Illfare in India*. Sage. NewDelhi.

Harris, John. 2002. *The Politics of Social Capital*. Leftword. New Delhi

Hart, Keith. 1999. *The Memory Bank:* Money in an Unequal World.

Ilean, Susan and Lynne Phillips, (2000) Mapping populations: the United Nations, Globalisation and Engendered Spaces, 1948-1960, *Alternatives*, 25(4): October-December 467-490.

Jaegar c. Carlo (1994), *Taming the Dragon: Transforming Economic institutions in the face of Global change*, Gordon and Preach, Switzerland.

Jones, C and Novak, T. (1999), *Poverty, Welfare and the disciplinary State.* RKP, London.

Jones, C and Novak, T. 1999. *Poverty, Welfare and the Disciplinary State.* RKP, London.

Jones, Chris, 1995. *The Ethics of Community Care*, RKP, London

Khor M (2000), Globalisation and the South: some critical issues, *Discussion Paper* No.147 UNCTAD, April.

Kothari, Uma and David Hulme, 2003. *Narratives, stories and tales: understanding poverty dynamics through life history.*

Laing, R.D. 1990. *The Politics of Experience.* London: Penguin Books Ltd.

Madely. J (1999), *Big Business, Poor Peoples*, Zed Books, London.

Mehta, Balraj (1990), "New Economic Policy: From Disenchantment to Discontent" in R.A Choudhury, Shama Gamkhar, Aurobindo Ghose (edited) *The Indian Economy and its Performance Since Independence*, Oxford University Press, New Delhi.

Michael & Nunn, P. 1994. *Paradox and Healing: Medicine, Mythology & Transformation*; Greenwood, Paradox Publishing.

Mills C. Wright. 1959 [1976] *The Sociological Imagination*. New York: Oxford University Press.

Mills, Wright C (1959), *The Sociological Imagination*; Oxford University Press.

Narayan, D, Chambers, R, Shah, M K, Petecsch, P. 2000b. *Voices of the Poor/; Crying out for Change*, Newyork . OUP.

Narayan, Deepa with Raj Patel, Kai Schafft, Anne Rademacher and Sarah Koch–Schulte. 2000. *Voices of the Poor: Can Anyone Hear Us?* New York, N.Y: Published for the World Bank, Oxford University Press

Pollis, A. 1992. 'Human Rights' in Mary Hawkesworth and Maurice Kogan (Eds) *Encyclopaedia of Government and Politics* Vol. 2. Routledge and Kegan Paul. London

Popper, Karl,1969. *Conjectures and Refutations*, Routledge, Routledge and Kegan Paul.

Ritzer G (1993), *The McDonoldization of Society*, Pine Forge Press.

Ruggeri Laderchi, Caterina 2001. *Participatory methods in the analysis of poverty: a critical review. QEH Working Paper Series* Working Paper Number 62

Sachs, Wolfgang (ed.); *The Development Dictionary: A Guide to Knowledge as Power.* - London [u.a.]: Zed Books [u.a.], 1992

Scott, James C. 1998. *Seeing Like a State: How Certain Schemes to Improve the Human Condition Have Failed.* Yale University Press.

Sheila Pelizzon and John Casparis (1996), "World Human Welfare" in Terence K. Hopkins and Immanuel Wallerstein edited *The Age of Transition*, Zed Books, London.

Slater, Rachel. 2000. 'Using Life Stories to Explore Change: Women's Urban Struggles in Cape Town, South Africa' in Gender and Life Cycles. Caroline Slater (ed); *Oxfam Focus On Gender*; Oxfam GB.

Slim and Thomson, 1993, *Listening for a Change*, Panos, London

Smith, Antony. S (2000), *Nationalism in Global Era*, Polity press UK, pp 147-159.

Strange S (1996), *The Retreat of the State*, Cambridge University Press, Cambridge.

Subramaniam and Harris, Barbara (Eds). 1999. *Illfare in India*. Sage. New Delhi.

Susan George (1976), *How The Other Half Dies?*, Harmondworth, London.

Trawick, Margaret, 1991."Wandering Lost: A Landless Labourer's Sense of Place and Self," in, Arjan Appadurai, Frank Korom, and Margaret Mills, (Eds). *Gender, Genre and Power in South Asian Expressive Traditions*, University of Pennsylvania Press.

REPORTS

Report of the Royal College of Psychiatrists, *Not just brick and Mortar*, January 1998

The Government's Response to the Health Select Committee's Report into Mental Health Services, 2000

www.ingramcontent.com/pod-product-compliance
Lightning Source LLC
Chambersburg PA
CBHW031106250726
48655CB00004B/1605